THE Saint
Benedict
PRAYER BOOK

Translated, adapted, and introduced by
JACOB RIYEFF, OblSB

Foreword by
FR. CASSIAN FOLSOM, OSB

PARACLETE PRESS
BREWSTER, MASSACHUSETTS

2021 First Printing

The Saint Benedict Prayer Book

Text copyright © 2021 by Jacob Riyeff

ISBN 978-1-64060-624-1

Library of Congress Cataloging-in-Publication Data

Names: Riyeff, Jacob, 1982- translator, adapter.

Title: The Saint Benedict prayer book / translated, adapted, and introduced by Jacob Riyeff, OblSB ; foreword by Fr. Cassian Folsom, OSB San Benedetto in Monte, Norcia, Italy.

Description: Brewster, Massachusetts : Paraclete Press, 2021. | Includes bibliographical references. | Summary: "A Benedictine prayer book reconnecting the treasures of liturgical and private prayer"-- Provided by publisher.

Identifiers: LCCN 2021006348 (print) | LCCN 2021006349 (ebook) | ISBN 9781640606241 | ISBN 9781640606258 (epub) | ISBN 9781640606265 (pdf)

Subjects: LCSH: Benedictines--Prayers and devotions. | Catholic Church--Prayers and devotions.

Classification: LCC BX2050.B46 S35 2021 (print) | LCC BX2050.B46 (ebook) | DDC 264/.15--dc23

LC record available at https://lccn.loc.gov/2021006348

LC ebook record available at https://lccn.loc.gov/2021006349

10 9 8 7 6 5 4 3 2 1

Published by Paraclete Press
Brewster, Massachusetts
www.paracletepress.com

Printed in the United States of America

FOREWORD

THIS DELIGHTFUL PRAYER BOOK IS UNIQUE, different from run-of-the-mill collections of prayers and devotions. It's as though the author went up into the attic of the tradition, searched among the treasure boxes there, and chose some of the best jewels to share with his friends.

It is a Benedictine prayer book that will also be enjoyed by those of a non-monastic persuasion, because it is deeply rooted in the liturgical life of the Church. The three main categories of texts are Little Offices (abbreviated forms of the Divine Office), Commemorations (additions to the Offices of Lauds and Vespers), and Litanies (an ever-popular form of devotional prayer).

A liturgically inspired prayer book like this can best be understood in a wider context: the perennial questions surrounding the relationship of private prayer and liturgical prayer. In the first millennium, when monks had finished chanting the Divine Office and wanted to continue to pray privately, they simply recited more psalms. This is an expression of enthusiasm and fervor. In the Carolingian period, when Saint Benedict of Aniane tried to trim back some of these luxurious extra-liturgical growths in order to return to the simplicity of the Rule of Saint Benedict, he met with stiff resistance. The monks wanted their devotions and would not part with them. Modern historians sometimes present this phenomenon as a collection of excessive and burdensome practices just waiting for reform, but that is anachronistic. Extra psalms, or collections of psalm verses, or additional antiphons—these were all elements of the ancient technique of *lectio divina*, mulling over the sacred text in order to memorize it and extract its nectar for the sweet honey of contemplation.

Later devotional history went in a different direction. The *Devotio Moderna* was precisely that: modern, emphasizing praiseworthy things such as meditation on the life of Christ, but by this time divorced from the liturgy. The Divine Office was often seen as an obligation to be dutifully carried out, but not as a source of spiritual nourishment. Even after the major overhaul of the post-Vatican II Liturgy of the Hours, and the widespread use of the vernacular, the tension remains.

The Saint Benedict Prayer Book is a fine example of the reconnection of liturgical and private prayer.

Monks, nuns, sisters, oblates, and non-monastics everywhere will find here a little treasure. Those not familiar with the monastic tradition of devotional prayer will make a wonderful new discovery.

FR. CASSIAN FOLSOM, OSB

San Benedetto in Monte
Norcia, Italy

CONTENTS

INTRODUCTION

F ROM THE EARLIEST DAYS OF THE CHURCH, Christians have celebrated with their words the great works God has done. Saint Paul says to "be filled with the Spirit, addressing one another [in] psalms and hymns and spiritual songs, singing and playing to the Lord in your hearts" (Eph. 5:18–19), while the author of the Letter to the Hebrews exhorts us to "continually offer God a sacrifice of praise" (Heb. 13:15).

From the beginning to today the words of the Scriptures and "inspired songs"—invoking lived experience in so many times and places and cultures—have given voice to individuals' and communities' thanks, praise, and reminders to stay on the Way (see Acts 9:2). Just as surely, early Church writers described how Christians also pray "beyond words," in the meditations of their hearts and the contemplation of heavenly realities. Origen, Evagrius, Saint Gregory Nazianzen, Saint John Cassian, Saint Benedict: these and many more taught that the most interior prayer passes beyond words and images, reaching to God himself. These early teachers saw both forms of prayer as helping and supporting each other, not as opposed to one another. Praying the psalms and singing hymns can provide us a whole spiritual vocabulary, can train the mind and heart to focus on what matters, and can give us durable images to hold and offer up in prayer. And the silences that come between the psalms, between the hymns, between the words, are just as important, just as pregnant—perhaps more so.

This book offers everyone and anyone a number of prayers from long ago—kinds of prayers that are now somewhat rare but were once the air that Christian communities breathed and that stood the test of centuries. These prayers come from the deep roots and flowering branches of the early Christian tradition. For hundreds of years, Christians who were trained in prayer turned especially to the psalms as to an unfailing spring of inspiration and refreshment, in the best and worst of times. As years passed, thematic verses, additional Scripture readings, and other elements were added to guide this prayer of the psalms for certain times of day, feast days, and devotions, forming what we call "the Liturgy of the Hours."

The monastic followers of Saint Benedict ("Benedictines") found the daily rounds of communal prayer of the Liturgy of the Hours so fruitful that they embellished and expanded them, adding other prayers that echoed the Hours' rhythmic and embodied way of praying. These forms of prayer, while sometimes unfamiliar to modern Christians, can still be great sources of spiritual nourishment, especially if they are paired with a mind attentive not only to the words but also to the quiet moments between the words, when the Spirit can intercede for us "with inexpressible groanings" (Rom. 8:26).

Saint Benedict says that the task of praying the psalms to God is so crucial to the Christian life that we should "consider . . . how we ought to behave in the presence of God and his angels" and "stand to sing the psalms in such a way that our minds are in harmony with our voices" (Rule of Saint Benedict 19.6–7).[1] The psalms and their spirituality are essential to the prayers offered here. Even those prayers that do not themselves contain the psalms are often intimately linked to them, because most are intended to adorn and resonate with the Liturgy of the Hours, whose very heart is the psalms. The

1 Timothy Fry, trans., *RB 1980: The Rule of Saint Benedict in Latin and English with Notes* (Collegeville, MN: Liturgical Press, 1981), Prologue.49. All following quotations of the Rule will appear as "RB" with the chapter and verse numbers for ease of reference.

repeated and rhythmic nature of these Hours trains the mind in attentiveness, attunes our whole being to the rhythms of the natural world, and urges us toward an expansive relationship with the divine.

Drawing on their resemblance to the Liturgy of the Hours, the prayers here can be thought of like an ornate set of jewelry. If the psalms are the gemstones, the different verses, hymns, and invocations of the Little Offices, Commemorations, and Litanies on the following pages are these precious stones' settings. They are not intended to take away from the brilliance of the gemstones, but rather to draw this brilliance out with their own luster. They do not rival the jewels' opulence but magnify it in their variety and accent it in their contrast. The disciples of Saint Benedict spent centuries developing and honing these prayers as they chanted the psalms in choir and muttered them as they went about their daily work. And we can now make them shine again for ourselves and others too as we make them from time to time our own "sacrifice of praise."

Benedictine Spirituality and the Liturgy of the Hours

Saint Benedict was born in Nursia (present day Norcia), Italy, around 480. Though sent to study in Rome so that he could become a well-educated nobleman, he was dismayed by the lax and depraved life in the city (nothing new under the sun!) and fled to seek a new life in the wilderness. After spending years as a hermit in a cave at Subiaco, Benedict eventually founded several monasteries—most famously the monastery at Monte Cassino near Rome. According to tradition, he worked many miracles and died praying in the presence of his disciples in 547.

While he never intended to form a "religious order," Benedict wrote a Rule for monks that has long been recognized as both a trusty practical guide for running a monastery and also a profound spiritual work. His monastic disciples, the Benedictines, dedicate themselves to a life lived in common, to persistent prayer, to silence, to hospitality, to a constant conversion of life, and to showing forth the goodness of God in all things. Benedictine spirituality is founded—paradoxically, on the surface—on the combination of obedience lived in community and on the intimate encounter with

God, the world, and oneself that is contemplation. The Benedictines have thrived, evolved, adapted, dwindled, and renewed themselves for around 1,500 years. Witnesses to the radical nature of humanity's search for God, Benedictines have, in their quiet and rhythmic way, continued the search and provided havens of silence and stillness for many others in the world along the way.

A special affection for the Liturgy and the psalms developed quickly in early monasticism and has remained a characteristic of monastic spirituality to the present day. "Chewing over" the Scriptures in the public liturgy and in private *lectio divina* (meditative reading of the Scriptures) has profoundly shaped monks and those who learn the spiritual life from them from the beginning, leading them to Christ with "hearts overflowing with the inexpressible delight of love" (RB Prol.49). This still happens. Benedict's Rule inspires monastics, and those who aspire to learn to pray like monastics, today.

In light of this tradition, Saint Benedict taught that the celebration of the Liturgy of the Hours was to be the primary act shaping the monk's spiritual life. Each daily "Hour" draws the Church together in communal offering of praise throughout the day to sanctify time. Saint Benedict found the Liturgy of the Hours so crucial that he went so far as to say that "nothing is to be preferred to" it (RB 43.3). This round of Hours then and now looks roughly like this:

MATINS (or Vigils, said in the night)

LAUDS (Morning Prayer)

PRIME (the morning office suppressed at Vatican II)

TERCE (Midmorning Prayer)

SEXT (Midday Prayer)

NONE (Midafternoon Prayer)

VESPERS (Evening Prayer)

COMPLINE (Night Prayer, before retiring)

This saturation of daily life with the Scriptures and the fruits of others' meditative reading prepares the seedbed of the soul for the fruits of meditation and contemplation.

Though approaching it can be intimidating or bewildering at first, clergy, monastics, and lay people today continue to pray the Liturgy of the Hours. In the Roman communion, the Liturgy of the Hours is available in English translation in a set of four books readily available in bookstores and online. The Anglican communion and Lutheran communion continue to celebrate the Hours with their own texts as well. With a little diligence and a hefty dose of patience, any Christian can learn to use ably these texts that are the Churches' daily offering to the Father, through the Son, in the Holy Spirit. Many lay people who take up the Hours pray them only occasionally, or they pray only Lauds and Vespers, or a similar selection. However one goes about it, any method of saying the Hours can help one perceive the rhythm of the Church's liturgical year more clearly and enter into the Church's own prayer more fully.

The monastics and clergy whom the Church demands pray the Liturgy of the Hours have fulfilled this obligation in different ways over the centuries. Early monastics recited all of the psalms in their cells daily. Early clergy who lived together in cathedrals began the first fully developed Hours with the verses and other prayers that shaped the daily meditation on the psalms. Monastics during the Middle Ages developed and expanded the Hours until in some monasteries most of a monk's day was spent in choir. After the Reformation, when new groups that were more engaged in active ministry (like the Jesuits and lay apostolates) developed, the full recitation of the Hours was limited. Today, many monastic communities say the most important Hours (Lauds and Vespers especially) together in choir and the "minor" Hours in their own rooms. The celebration and obligations have changed over the course of history, but the centrality of the Liturgy of the Hours in the Church's prayer life has not.

The most important development in the celebration of the Liturgy of the Hours for this book is how monastics throughout the Middle Ages made "additions" to the Hours. These additional prayers were made to resemble the Hours, but they show much greater freedom as well. Through them, monks sought to bring the prayer of the Liturgy even closer to the private prayer of ordinary people. In the special prayers included in this book the official prayers of the Liturgy and the individual prayers of the saints (see Rev. 8:4) draw, ideally, into a seamless unity.

Benedictine scholar Jean Leclercq once called the Liturgy of the Hours a poem.[2] In our day, when poems have returned to the special place they once held as conveyors of spiritual wisdom, this metaphor is particularly apt.

2 Jean Leclercq, *The Love of Learning and the Desire for God: A Study of Monastic Culture* (New York: Fordham University Press, 1982), 236.

Like a poem, the Liturgy of the Hours is composed of words. Like a poem, the Liturgy of the Hours relies on images, figures of speech, and the rhythm and sound of words together to convey its meaning. Perhaps less obviously, and still like a poem, the Liturgy of the Hours "thinks" through association and intuition rather than through formal logic. Like a poem, the Liturgy of the Hours is more concerned with leading and guiding and forming the heart than in making a clear intellectual point. Like a poem, the Liturgy of the Hours aspires to be beautiful and pregnant with meaning. And like a poem, the Liturgy of the Hours begs to be *performed*.

Think of the prayers in this book as spiritual poems in this way. Because they are so intimately related to the Hours, a similar way of teaching wisdom undergirds them. They are all poetic offerings to the One from whom they've come. They call us to attentiveness to God's ways, to his pervasive presence in our lives and in the world, to the rhythms of the natural world and the Church's liturgical year, and to the unity of the individual, the larger Church, and the entire created order with their Creator.

In practice, these prayers can be used in any number of ways. One might pray "The Little Office of the Trinity" on Trinity Sunday, or every Sunday.[3] One might pray "The Little Office of the Cross" on Good Friday, or every Friday. The offices and litanies of different saints might be said on their feast days. If one prays Lauds and Vespers regularly, the Commemorations might be said after them on certain set days, or as an extra practice during Lent. Because most of these prayers are "hooked" to certain times, devotions, or saints, but not in any restrictive way, they can be readily adapted to anyone's needs.

However they are used, every prayer and liturgy in this book is intended to support those who care about ancient ways of praying, to provide traditional prayers for those who practice monastic spirituality, and to more perfectly realize "the relation between the liturgy and the whole of Christian life" as "the prayer of the [Liturgy of the Hours] becomes" evermore our "genuine personal prayer."[4]

---

3 "Office" is another word for "Hour," the group of prayers said at a set period of time.
4 The Sacred Congregation for Divine Worship, "Laudis Canticum," in *The Liturgy of the Hours*, vol. 1, 18.

The Different Types of Benedictine Prayer[5]

Little Offices

Our first group of prayers are Little Offices, which began to form in the early ninth century with the Office of the Dead. Not all these practices and devotions were public—in other words, they were largely unknown outside Benedictine monasteries. The first of them that survive are from eleventh-century Winchester, England, and found in a book that belonged to a Benedictine abbot named Ælfwine. These earliest Little Offices are the first three in this book. By the tenth and eleventh century, the structure of psalms, antiphons,[6] readings, versicles and responses,[7] and collects[8] seems to be the air that monks breathed as they

---

5 Many of the specifics in this section come from Sally Elizabeth Roper's excellent book *Medieval English Benedictine Liturgy: Studies in the Formation, Structure, and Content of the Monastic Votive Office, c. 950-1540* (New York: Garland Publishing, 1993).

6 "Antiphon" is the word for a short refrain recited before and after a psalm or canticle.

7 "Versicle" is the word for a short verse recited by the leader of a prayer, while the "Response" is the short verse said by everyone else present in response to the versicle. (When reciting prayers alone, one says/prays both the Versicle and Response.)

8 "Collect" is the word for brief prayers recited at the Mass and at the Liturgy of the Hours, having an invocation, a petition, and a conclusion.

prayed. So, when abbots suggested private prayers to their monks, the prayers looked very much like the daily Hours they all recited together.

Each Little Office can be said at any time of year, but some days or seasons will seem more fitting. For monastics and oblates, the Little Office of Saint Benedict might become a weekly observance said after the regular Hours (Tuesday was often a day when this office was recited in the past), or it might be a special devotion on his feast days. The other saints' offices could be said after the Liturgy of the Hours on their feast days, or if a special intention is being prayed for.

Commemorations

Next, you will find prayers called Commemorations. Commemorations are short prayers made up of an antiphon, a versicle and response, and a collect prayer, but no psalms. Each Commemoration is said in honor of God, a saint, or a particular intention. They were traditionally said after Lauds and Vespers. These prayers may have had their origin in the prayers for absent monks that Benedict calls for in his Rule (RB 67.2). The Commemorations you will find here come from a Book of Hours used by the monks of Winchester Cathedral Priory and have been reduced and streamlined for ease of praying. The idea behind these prayers is to linger awhile after the Hours are finished, to offer praise and thanksgiving in a focused way that goes above and beyond the official liturgy.

Litanies

The Litanies in the next group are probably more familiar to most people than Little Offices and Commemorations. The Litany form of prayer came to the West by at least the seventh century and usually attended processions during liturgical celebrations and in times of calamity such as famine, earthquake, or a lack of rain. For example, if a famine occurred, a community might process together from one church to another while reciting the Litany of Saints and praying for an end to the disaster. By the twelfth century, Litanies directed to Saint Mary were circulating, and after the sixteenth century, Litanies proliferated for different devotions and to different saints.

The repetitive nature of Litanies contributed to their popularity—in a way that might be less appreciated today. Perhaps we might rediscover this prayer form and what it offers us. The repetition of phrases along with variations that make up a Litany can appeal to our sense of rhythm and music. This in turn creates a sense of language use that is "different" from the everyday. This is apparent in individual recitation but becomes even clearer when a group recites a Litany together. The call-and-response is an ancient technique for song and prayer from all over the world. All the Litanies included here are intended for private prayer, whether alone or in a small group, and are dedicated to different Benedictine saints. As we pray these Litanies, we can use their repetitive structure to carve out time for meditation on the lives of our predecessors in faith and gain insight into their virtues through the images they offer us.

Finally, in the last section, there are brief prayers collected from very different sources, all oriented around Saint Benedict or Benedictine life in one way or another. These prayers are just a few of the many present in a large store of sources that can inspire us with new ways to relate to the patriarch of Western monasticism, give a sense of the rich tradition of Benedictine prayer from a millennium and a half of monastic experience, and help prepare the body, mind, and soul for meditative and contemplative prayer.

A Note on Translation

All translations included here are my own, except the translations of Psalms and Readings (which are taken from the 1914 Douay version, with alterations, and *The New American Bible, Revised Edition*, respectively) and traditional prayers such as the "Glory be," etc.

LITTLE OFFICES

THE LITTLE OFFICE OF
THE TRINITY

(🐚) *This beautiful offering to the Blessed Trinity focuses our attention on the central mystery of Who God Is. From one view, Christian history is the history of people wrestling with Saint John's teaching that "God is love" (1 John 4:8, 16)—not that God loves us (though he does!), but that God is Love itself. In being a perfect communion of Persons, the source and goal of all things is Love perfectly poured out in self-gift. This office focuses us on this great revelation, which we still have yet to plumb fully after two millennia. Its recitation would be most appropriate on Trinity Sunday, but all times are appropriate for this fundamental act of Christian worship—giving glory to the Father and the Son and the Holy Spirit. Depending on whether you say the office or chant it, you might want to set aside around 10–15 minutes to pray this office.*

Versicle: God, come to my assistance.
Response: Lord, make haste to help me.

Glory be to the Father and to the Son and to the Holy Spirit.
As it was in the beginning, is now, and ever shall be, world without end. Amen.

Antiphon: O beatific and blessèd and glorious
Trinity, Father, Son, and Holy Spirit: to you be
praise, glory, and thanksgiving.

PSALM 54

Save me, O God, by your name,
and judge me in your strength.
O God, hear my prayer;
give ear to the words of my mouth.
For strangers have risen up against me,
and the mighty have sought after my soul,
and they have not set God before their eyes.
For, behold, God is my helper,
and the Lord is the protector of my soul.
Turn back the evils upon my enemies
and cut them off in your truth.
I will freely sacrifice to you
and will give praise, O God, to your name,
because it is good.
For you have delivered me out of all trouble,
and my eye has looked down upon my enemies.

Glory be to the Father . . .

Antiphon: O beatific and blesséd and glorious
Trinity, Father, Son, and Holy Spirit: to you be
praise, glory, and thanksgiving.

PSALM 118

Give praise to the Lord, for he is good,
for his mercy endures for ever.
Let Israel now say that he is good,
that his mercy endures for ever.
Let the house of Aaron now say
that his mercy endures for ever.
Let them that fear the Lord now say
that his mercy endures for ever.
In my trouble I called upon the Lord,
and the Lord heard me and enlarged me.
The Lord is my helper;
I will not fear what man can do unto me.
The Lord is my helper,
and I will look over my enemies.
It is good to confide in the Lord
rather than to have confidence in man.
It is good to trust in the Lord
rather than to trust in princes.
All nations compassed me about,
and in the name of the Lord I have been revenged
  on them.

Surrounding me they compassed me about,
and in the name of the Lord I have been revenged
   on them.
They surrounded me like bees,
and they burned like fire among thorns,
and in the name of the Lord I was revenged on
   them.
Being pushed I was overturned that I might fall,
but the Lord supported me.
The Lord is my strength and my praise,
and he is become my salvation.
The voice of rejoicing and of salvation
is in the tents of the just.
The right hand of the Lord has wrought strength;
the right hand of the Lord has exalted me;
the right hand of the Lord has wrought strength.
I shall not die, but live
and shall declare the works of the Lord.
The Lord chastising has chastised me,
but he has not delivered me over to death.
Open to me the gates of justice.
I will go in to them, and give praise to the Lord.
This is the gate of the Lord,
the just shall enter into it.
I will give glory to you,
because you have heard me,

and are become my salvation.
The stone which the builders rejected,
the same is become the cornerstone.
This is the Lord's doing,
and it is wonderful in our eyes.
This is the day which the Lord has made;
let us be glad and rejoice therein.
O Lord, save me; O Lord, give good success.
Blessed be he that comes in the name of the Lord.
We have blessed you out of the house of the Lord.
The Lord is God, and he has shone upon us.
Appoint a solemn day, with shady boughs,
even to the horn of the altar.
You are my God, and I will praise you.
You are my God, and I will exalt you.
I will praise you, because you have heard me,
and are become my salvation.
O praise the Lord, for he is good,
for his mercy endures for ever.

Glory be to the Father . . .

Antiphon: O beatific and blessèd and glorious
Trinity, Father, Son, and Holy Spirit: to you be
praise, glory, and thanksgiving.

Psalm 8[9]

O Lord our Lord, how admirable
is your name in the whole earth!
For your magnificence is elevated
above the heavens.
Out of the mouth of infants and of those at the
 breast,
you have perfected praise,
because of your enemies,
that you may destroy the enemy and the avenger.
For I will behold your heavens,
the works of your fingers:
the moon and the stars
which you have founded.
What is man that you are mindful of him?
or the son of man that you visit him?
You have made him a little less than the angels,
you have crowned him with glory and honor,
and have set him over the works of your hands.
You have subjected all things under his feet,
all sheep and oxen,
moreover the beasts also of the fields,
the birds of the air, and the fishes of the sea

9 The manuscript calls here for Psalm 119, the great
 meditation on the Law, but given how long it is, I have
 provided Psalm 8, a much shorter psalm that is used in
 the modern office of Trinity Sunday.

that pass through the paths of the sea.
O Lord our Lord, how admirable
is your name in all the earth!

Hymn   TE DECET LAUS[10]
It is right to praise you;
it is right to sing hymns to you.
Glory to you:
God the Father and the Son
with the Holy Spirit,
world without end. Amen.

Antiphon: O beatific and blessèd and glorious
Trinity, Father, Son, and Holy Spirit: to you be
praise, glory, and thanksgiving.

Reading   1 JOHN 5:7–8
So there are three that testify, the Spirit, the water,
and the blood, and the three are of one accord.

10 The manuscript calls here for the Athanasian Creed, a
   statement of Trinitarian and Incarnational belief. Due
   to the fact that this creed has been all but abandoned
   in the current Roman Rite, and due to its length and its
   tone, I have provided the *Te Decet Laus*, a much shorter
   statement of Trinitarian belief from the monastic Hours.

Versicle: May God our God bless us, may God bless us, and may all the ends of the earth tremble before him.

Response: May God have mercy on us, and may God bless us, and may all the ends of the earth tremble before him.

Hymn   VENI CREATOR SPIRITUS
                    (trans. by Robert Bridges)

Come, O Creator Spirit, come,
and make within our heart thy home;
to us thy grace celestial give,
who of thy breathing move and live.

O Comforter, that name is thine,
of God most high the gift divine;
the well of life, the fire of love,
our souls' anointing from above.

Thou dost appear in sevenfold dower
the sign of God's almighty power;
the Father's promise, making rich
with saving truth our earthly speech.

Our senses with thy light inflame,
our hearts to heav'nly love reclaim;
our bodies' poor infirmity
with strength perpetual fortify.

Our mortal foes afar repel,
grant us henceforth in peace to dwell;
and so to us, with thee for guide,
no ill shall come, no harm betide.

May we by thee the Father learn,
and know the Son, and thee discern,
who art of both; and thus adore
in perfect faith for evermore. Amen.

Versicle: May the name of the Lord be blessed.
Response: Both now and forever.

Antiphon: We confess you with our whole hearts
and our mouths, unbegotten Father, only begotten
Son, and Holy Spirit the Paraclete, holy and
undivided Trinity; we praise you and we bless you,
and we give you glory forever.

MAGNIFICAT[11]

My soul proclaims the greatness of the Lord;
my spirit rejoices in God my savior.
For he has looked upon his handmaid's lowliness;
behold, from now on will all ages call me blessed.
The Mighty One has done great things for me,
and holy is his name.

11 Traditionally, the Sign of the Cross is made when
   beginning the Magnificat.

His mercy is from age to age
to those who fear him.
He has shown might with his arm,
dispersed the arrogant of mind and heart.
He has thrown down the rulers from their thrones
but lifted up the lowly.
The hungry he has filled with good things;
the rich he has sent away empty.
He has helped Israel his servant,
remembering his mercy,
according to his promise to our fathers,
to Abraham and to his descendants forever.

Glory be to the Father . . .

Antiphon: We confess you with our whole hearts
and our mouths, unbegotten Father, only begotten
Son, and Holy Spirit the Paraclete, holy and
undivided Trinity; we praise you and we bless you,
and we give you glory forever.

Kyrie eleison. Christe eleison. Kyrie eleison.

Our Father . . .

I believe in one God . . .

Versicle: Let us bless the Father and the Son and the Holy Spirit.

Response: Blessed are you Lord; teach me your statutes.

PRAYERS

May the exalted and undivided Trinity, Father, Son, and Holy Spirit, bless and guard us and drive all sinful deeds far from us. Holy and undivided Trinity, relying on you we ask that you blot out the shame of your servants and preserve us in your service.

May the all-powerful God, who made heaven and earth, the seas and all they contain, bless and guard us.

May the holy Trinity and undivided Unity be blessed, may we confess him, that he might show us his mercy.

O beatific and blesséd and glorious Trinity, Father, Son, and Holy Spirit: praise, glory, thanks, honor, power, and strength be to you our God forever.

Exalted and only Deity, we ask that you might absolve us of our sins, remove our faults, and grant peace to your servants, so that we might give you glory in all things forever.

Psalm 143

Hear, O Lord, my prayer;
give ear to my supplication in your truth;
hear me in your justice.
And enter not into judgment with your servant,
for in your sight no man living shall be justified.
For the enemy has persecuted my soul.
He has brought down my life to the earth.
He has made me to dwell in darkness
as those that have been dead of old.
And my spirit is in anguish within me,
my heart within me is troubled.
I remembered the days of old,
I meditated on all your works,
I meditated upon the works of your hands.
I stretched forth my hands to you;
my soul is as earth without water unto you.
Hear me speedily, O Lord,
my spirit has fainted away.
Turn not away your face from me,
lest I be like unto them that go down into the pit.

Cause me to hear your mercy in the morning,
for in you have I hoped.
Make the way known to me wherein I should walk,
for I have lifted up my soul to you.
Deliver me from my enemies,
O Lord, to you I have fled.
Teach me to do your will,
for you are my God.
Your good spirit shall lead me into the right land.
For your name's sake, O Lord, you will quicken me
in your justice.
You will bring my soul out of trouble,
and in your mercy you will destroy my enemies.
And you will cut off all them that afflict my soul,
for I am your servant.

Prayer

Almighty and eternal God, co-eternal majesty and only Deity, you who persist in Trinity and remain in Unity: grant, we beseech you, that we who are weighed down by our sins might obtain pardon through your swift kindness. Through Christ our Lord. Amen.

THE LITTLE OFFICE OF
OUR LADY

Christians have turned to Jesus's mother in prayer for help and comfort in tribulations and in daily life from the early centuries of the Church. We exalt Mary because of her role in Christ's Incarnation but also because of her model discipleship. In this office, Mary's divine motherhood is called to mind most often. But it also makes clear her "queenship" and ability to help Christians in dire situations, so turning to this prayer for any particularly pressing problems, spiritual or temporal, is most appropriate. This office could be recited on Saturdays (the day traditionally associated with Mary) and especially on her various feast days. Depending on whether you say the office or chant it, you might want to set aside around 10–15 minutes to pray this office.

Versicle: God, come to my assistance.
Response: Lord, make haste to help me.

Glory be to the Father and to the Son and to the Holy Spirit.
As it was in the beginning, is now, and ever shall be, world without end. Amen.

Antiphon: Hail Mary, full of grace, the Lord is with you; blessed are you among women, alleluia.

PSALM 54

Save me, O God, by your name,
and judge me in your strength.
O God, hear my prayer;
give ear to the words of my mouth.
For strangers have risen up against me,
and the mighty have sought after my soul,
and they have not set God before their eyes.
For, behold, God is my helper,
and the Lord is the protector of my soul.
Turn back the evils upon my enemies
and cut them off in your truth.
I will freely sacrifice to you
and will give praise, O God, to your name,
because it is good.
For you have delivered me out of all trouble,
and my eye has looked down upon my enemies.

Glory be to the Father . . .

Antiphon: Hail Mary, full of grace, the Lord is with you; blessed are you among women, alleluia.

PSALM 118

Give praise to the Lord, for he is good,
for his mercy endures for ever.
Let Israel now say that he is good,
that his mercy endures for ever.
Let the house of Aaron now say
that his mercy endures for ever.
Let them that fear the Lord now say
that his mercy endures for ever.
In my trouble I called upon the Lord,
and the Lord heard me and enlarged me.
The Lord is my helper;
I will not fear what man can do unto me.
The Lord is my helper,
and I will look over my enemies.
It is good to confide in the Lord
rather than to have confidence in man.
It is good to trust in the Lord
rather than to trust in princes.
All nations compassed me about,
and in the name of the Lord I have been revenged
    on them.
Surrounding me they compassed me about,
and in the name of the Lord I have been revenged
    on them.

They surrounded me like bees,

and they burned like fire among thorns,

and in the name of the Lord I was revenged on them.

Being pushed I was overturned that I might fall,

but the Lord supported me.

The Lord is my strength and my praise,

and he is become my salvation.

The voice of rejoicing and of salvation

is in the tents of the just.

The right hand of the Lord has wrought strength;

the right hand of the Lord has exalted me;

the right hand of the Lord has wrought strength.

I shall not die, but live

and shall declare the works of the Lord.

The Lord chastising has chastised me,

but he has not delivered me over to death.

Open to me the gates of justice.

I will go in to them, and give praise to the Lord.

This is the gate of the Lord,

the just shall enter into it.

I will give glory to you,

because you have heard me,

and are become my salvation.

The stone which the builders rejected,

the same is become the cornerstone.

This is the Lord's doing,
and it is wonderful in our eyes.
This is the day which the Lord has made;
let us be glad and rejoice therein.
O Lord, save me; O Lord, give good success.
Blessed be he that comes in the name of the Lord.
We have blessed you out of the house of the Lord.
The Lord is God, and he has shone upon us.
Appoint a solemn day, with shady boughs,
even to the horn of the altar.
You are my God, and I will praise you.
You are my God, and I will exalt you.
I will praise you, because you have heard me,
and are become my salvation.
O praise the Lord, for he is good,
for his mercy endures for ever.

Glory be to the Father . . .

Antiphon: Hail Mary, full of grace, the Lord is with you; blessed are you among women, alleluia.

The foundations thereof are in the holy mountains:
the Lord loves the gates of Zion
above all the tabernacles of Jacob.
Glorious things are said of you,
O city of God.
I will be mindful of Rahab
and of Babylon knowing me.
Behold the foreigners, and Tyre
and the people of the Ethiopians,
these were there.
Shall not Zion say: This man and that man is born
   in her?
and the Highest himself has founded her.
The Lord shall tell in his writings
of peoples and princes,
of them that have been in her.
The dwelling in you
is as it were of all rejoicing.

12 The manuscript calls here for Psalm 119, the great
   meditation on the Law, but given how long it is, I have
   provided Psalm 87 instead, a shorter psalm that is used
   in the modern office for the Blessed Virgin Mary and
   alludes to Mary's divine motherhood.

Hymn Te Decet Laus[13]

It is right to praise you;
it is right to sing hymns to you.
Glory to you:
God the Father and the Son
with the Holy Spirit,
world without end. Amen.

Glory be to the Father . . .

Antiphon: Hail Mary, full of grace, the Lord is with
you; blessed are you among women, alleluia.

Reading Sirach 24:9–10

Before all ages, from the beginning, he created me,
and through all ages I shall not cease to be.
In the holy tent I ministered before him.

13 The manuscript calls here for the Athanasian Creed, a
statement of Trinitarian and Incarnational belief. Due
to the fact that this creed has been all but abandoned
in the current Roman Rite, and due to its length and its
tone, I have provided the *Te Decet Laus*, a much shorter
statement of Trinitarian belief from the monastic office.

Versicle: Blessed are you, Mary, who carried the Creator of all things; you gave birth to God who made you and remain a virgin forever.

Response: Hail Mary, full of grace, the Lord is with you; you gave birth to God who made you and remain a virgin forever.

Hymn   AVE MARIS STELLA
               (trans. by Anonymous)

Bright Mother of our Maker, hail,
thou virgin ever blest,
the ocean's star by which we sail,
and gain the port of rest.

Whilst we this *Ave* thus to thee
from Gabriel's mouth rehearse:
prevail that peace our lot may be,
and Eva's name reverse.

Release our long-entangled mind,
from all the snares of ill;
with heavenly light instruct the blind,
and all our vows fulfill.

Exert for us a mother's care,
and us thy children own.
Prevail with him to hear our prayer,
who chose to be thy son.

O spotless maid! whose virtues shine
with brightest purity:
each action of our lives refine,
and make us pure like thee.

Preserve our lives unstained with ill
in this infectious way,
that heaven alone our souls may fill
with joys that ne'er decay.

To God the Father endless praise,
to God the Son the same,
and Holy Ghost, whose equal rays
one equal glory claim. Amen.

Versicle: After childbirth you remained a Virgin.
Response: Mother of God, intercede for us.

Antiphon: Succor, holy mother of Christ, the wretched who flee to you; help and comfort all who trust in you; pray for the sins of all the world; intervene for the clergy, intercede for the choir of monks, plead for women.

MAGNIFICAT[14]

My soul proclaims the greatness of the Lord;
my spirit rejoices in God my savior.
For he has looked upon his handmaid's lowliness;
behold, from now on will all ages call me blessed.
The Mighty One has done great things for me,
and holy is his name.
His mercy is from age to age
to those who fear him.
He has shown might with his arm,
dispersed the arrogant of mind and heart.
He has thrown down the rulers from their thrones
but lifted up the lowly.
The hungry he has filled with good things;
the rich he has sent away empty.
He has helped Israel his servant,
remembering his mercy,
according to his promise to our fathers,
to Abraham and to his descendants forever.

Glory be to the Father . . .

14 Traditionally, the Sign of the Cross is made when
   beginning the Magnificat.

Antiphon: Succor, holy mother of Christ, the wretched who flee to you; help and comfort all who trust in you; pray for the sins of all the world; intervene for the clergy, intercede for the choir of monks, plead for women.

Kyrie eleison. Christe eleison. Kyrie eleison.

Our Father . . .

I believe in one God . . .

Versicle: Blessed Mother and unwed Virgin, glorious Queen of the world, intercede for us with the Lord.
Response: After childbirth you remained a Virgin; Mother of God, intercede for us.

PRAYERS

Hail Mary, full of grace, the Lord is with you; blessed are you among women.

With your splendor and your beauty, set out, proceed prosperously, and reign.

PSALM 143

Hear, O Lord, my prayer;
give ear to my supplication in your truth;
hear me in your justice.
And enter not into judgment with your servant,
for in your sight no man living shall be justified.
For the enemy has persecuted my soul.
He has brought down my life to the earth.
He has made me to dwell in darkness
as those that have been dead of old.
And my spirit is in anguish within me,
my heart within me is troubled.
I remembered the days of old,
I meditated on all your works,
I meditated upon the works of your hands.
I stretched forth my hands to you;
my soul is as earth without water unto you.
Hear me speedily, O Lord,
my spirit has fainted away.
Turn not away your face from me,
lest I be like unto them that go down into the pit.
Cause me to hear your mercy in the morning,
for in you have I hoped.
Make the way known to me wherein I should walk,
for I have lifted up my soul to you.

Deliver me from my enemies,
O Lord, to you I have fled.
Teach me to do your will,
for you are my God.
Your good spirit shall lead me into the right land.
For your name's sake, O Lord, you will quicken me
     in your justice.
You will bring my soul out of trouble,
and in your mercy you will destroy my enemies.
And you will cut off all them that afflict my soul,
for I am your servant.

PRAYER

Having propitiated you, Lord, avert, we beseech you, your anger from us, and drive out our sinful deeds through which we have provoked your indignation. Through Christ our Lord. Amen.

THE LITTLE OFFICE OF
THE CROSS

This office is ideal for calling to mind God's lavish generosity as well as Christ's solidarity with us in our sorrow and suffering. From the early centuries of the Church, especially in the West, devotion to Christ's crucifixion and the Cross itself highlighted God's great humbling of himself for the sake of a humanity lost in sin. This devotion grew to a fevered pitch in the later Middle Ages, but its relevance and beauty are still highlighted in devotions like the Good Friday liturgy, the Way of the Cross, the crucifix, and the Sorrowful Mysteries of the Rosary. When we experience our own suffering or we want to express thanksgiving for God's suffering and death that we might have life, this office focuses us on a concrete symbol of that sacrificial love. This office could be recited on Fridays (the day traditionally associated with the Passion) and especially on the Triumph of the Cross (September 14th), Passion Sunday, and Good Friday. Depending on whether you say the office or chant it, you might want to set aside around 10–15 minutes to pray this office.

Versicle: God, come to my assistance.

Response: Lord, make haste to help me.

Glory be to the Father and to the Son and to the Holy Spirit.

As it was in the beginning, is now, and ever shall be, world without end. Amen.

Antiphon: Save us, Christ our Savior, through the power of your Cross; you who saved Peter on the sea, have mercy on us.

PSALM 54

Save me, O God, by your name,
and judge me in your strength.
O God, hear my prayer;
give ear to the words of my mouth.
For strangers have risen up against me,
and the mighty have sought after my soul,
and they have not set God before their eyes.
For, behold, God is my helper,
and the Lord is the protector of my soul.
Turn back the evils upon my enemies
and cut them off in your truth.
I will freely sacrifice to you
and will give praise, O God, to your name,
because it is good.

For you have delivered me out of all trouble,
and my eye has looked down upon my enemies.

Glory be to the Father . . .

Antiphon: Save us, Christ our Savior, through the
power of your Cross; you who saved Peter on the
sea, have mercy on us.

PSALM 118

Give praise to the Lord, for he is good,
for his mercy endures for ever.
Let Israel now say that he is good,
that his mercy endures for ever.
Let the house of Aaron now say
that his mercy endures for ever.
Let them that fear the Lord now say
that his mercy endures for ever.
In my trouble I called upon the Lord,
and the Lord heard me and enlarged me.
The Lord is my helper;
I will not fear what man can do unto me.
The Lord is my helper,
and I will look over my enemies.
It is good to confide in the Lord
rather than to have confidence in man.

It is good to trust in the Lord
rather than to trust in princes.
All nations compassed me about,
and in the name of the Lord I have been revenged
on them.
Surrounding me they compassed me about,
and in the name of the Lord I have been revenged
on them.
They surrounded me like bees,
and they burned like fire among thorns,
and in the name of the Lord I was revenged on
them.
Being pushed I was overturned that I might fall,
but the Lord supported me.
The Lord is my strength and my praise,
and he is become my salvation.
The voice of rejoicing and of salvation
is in the tents of the just.
The right hand of the Lord has wrought strength;
the right hand of the Lord has exalted me;
the right hand of the Lord has wrought strength.
I shall not die, but live
and shall declare the works of the Lord.
The Lord chastising has chastised me,
but he has not delivered me over to death.
Open to me the gates of justice.

I will go in to them, and give praise to the Lord.
This is the gate of the Lord,
the just shall enter into it.
I will give glory to you,
because you have heard me,
and are become my salvation.
The stone which the builders rejected,
the same is become the cornerstone.
This is the Lord's doing,
and it is wonderful in our eyes.
This is the day which the Lord has made;
let us be glad and rejoice therein.
O Lord, save me; O Lord, give good success.
Blessed be he that comes in the name of the Lord.
We have blessed you out of the house of the Lord.
The Lord is God, and he has shone upon us.
Appoint a solemn day, with shady boughs,
even to the horn of the altar.
You are my God, and I will praise you.
You are my God, and I will exalt you.
I will praise you, because you have heard me,
and are become my salvation.
O praise the Lord, for he is good,
for his mercy endures for ever.

Glory be to the Father . . .

Antiphon: Save us, Christ our Savior, through the power of your Cross; you who saved Peter on the sea, have mercy on us.

PSALM 2[15]

Why have the nations raged,
and the people devised vain things?
The kings of the earth stood up,
and the princes met together,
against the Lord and against his Christ.
Let us break their bonds asunder,
and let us cast away their yoke from us.
He that dwells in heaven shall laugh at them,
and the Lord shall deride them.
Then shall he speak to them in his anger,
and trouble them in his rage.
But I am appointed king by him
over Zion his holy mountain,
preaching his commandment.
The Lord has said to me:
"You are my son, this day have I begotten you.

---

15 The manuscript calls here for Psalm 119, the great
   meditation on the Law, but given how long it is, I have
   provided Psalm 2, one of the psalms that prophesies
   the Messiah and is used in the modern office for the
   Triumph of the Cross.

Ask of me, and I will give you the nations for your
   inheritance,
and the utmost parts of the earth for your
   possession.
You shall rule them with a rod of iron
and shall break them in pieces like a potter's vessel."
And now, O you kings, understand:
receive instruction, you that judge the earth.
Serve the Lord with fear
and rejoice unto him with trembling.
Embrace discipline, lest at any time the Lord be
   angry,
and you perish from the just way.
When his wrath shall be kindled in a short time,
blessed are all they that trust in him.

Hymn   TE DECET LAUS[16]

It is right to praise you;
it is right to sing hymns to you.
Glory to you:
God the Father and the Son
with the Holy Spirit,
world without end. Amen.

Glory be to the Father . . .

Antiphon: Save us, Christ our Savior, through the power of your Cross; you who saved Peter on the sea, have mercy on us.

Reading   1 PETER 2:24

He himself bore our sins in his body upon the cross, so that, free from sin, we might live for righteousness. By his wounds you have been healed.

---

16 The manuscript calls here for the Athanasian Creed, a statement of Trinitarian and Incarnational belief. Due to the fact that this creed has been all but abandoned in the current Roman Rite, its length, and its tone, I have provided the *Te Decet Laus*, a much shorter statement of Trinitarian belief from the monastic office.

Versicle: O blessed Cross, which alone was worthy to bear the King and Lord of heaven.

Response: O admirable Cross, purging of injury, restoration of health, which alone was worthy to bear the King and Lord of heaven.

Hymn   VEXILLA REGIS
                   (trans. by Walter Kirkham Blount)

Abroad the regal banners fly,
now shines the Cross's mystery:
upon it Life did death endure,
and yet by death did life procure.

Who, wounded with a direful spear,
did purposely to wash us clear
from stain of sin, pour out a flood
of precious water mixed with blood.

That which the prophet-king of old
hath in mysterious verse foretold,
is now accomplished, whilst we see
God ruling the nations from a Tree.

O lovely and refulgent Tree,
adorned with purple majesty;
culled from a worthy stock to bear
those limbs which sanctiféd were.

Blest Tree, whose happy branches bore
the wealth that did the world restore;
the beam that did that body weigh
which raised up hell's expected prey.

Versicle: All the world adores you, God.
Response: And sings psalms to you.

Antiphon: You alone excel all the woods of cedar:
upon which hung the life of the world, upon which
Christ triumphed and death overcame death,
alleluia.

MAGNIFICAT[17]

My soul proclaims the greatness of the Lord;
my spirit rejoices in God my savior.
For he has looked upon his handmaid's lowliness;
behold, from now on will all ages call me blessed.
The Mighty One has done great things for me,
and holy is his name.
His mercy is from age to age
to those who fear him.
He has shown might with his arm,
dispersed the arrogant of mind and heart.

17 Traditionally, the Sign of the Cross is made when
beginning the Magnificat.

He has thrown down the rulers from their thrones
but lifted up the lowly.
The hungry he has filled with good things;
the rich he has sent away empty.
He has helped Israel his servant,
remembering his mercy,
according to his promise to our fathers,
to Abraham and to his descendants forever.

Antiphon: You alone excel all the woods of cedar: upon which hung the life of the world, upon which Christ triumphed and death overcame death, alleluia.

Kyrie eleison. Christe eleison. Kyrie eleison.

Our Father . . .

I believe in one God . . .

Versicle: We adore you, Christ, and we bless you, for by your holy Cross you have redeemed the world.
Response: This sign of the holy Cross will appear in the sky when the Lord comes for Judgment.

Proclaim to the nations, for the Lord has ruled
   from the wood.

We adore your Cross, Lord, and we recall your
   glorious Passion.

PSALM 143

Hear, O Lord, my prayer;
give ear to my supplication in your truth;
hear me in your justice.
And enter not into judgment with your servant,
for in your sight no man living shall be justified.
For the enemy has persecuted my soul.
He has brought down my life to the earth.
He has made me to dwell in darkness
as those that have been dead of old.
And my spirit is in anguish within me,
my heart within me is troubled.
I remembered the days of old,
I meditated on all your works,
I meditated upon the works of your hands.
I stretched forth my hands to you;
my soul is as earth without water unto you.
Hear me speedily, O Lord,
my spirit has fainted away.

Turn not away your face from me,
lest I be like unto them that go down into the pit.
Cause me to hear your mercy in the morning,
for in you have I hoped.
Make the way known to me wherein I should walk,
for I have lifted up my soul to you.
Deliver me from my enemies,
O Lord, to you I have fled.
Teach me to do your will,
for you are my God.
Your good spirit shall lead me into the right land.
For your name's sake, O Lord, you will quicken me
  in your justice.
You will bring my soul out of trouble,
and in your mercy you will destroy my enemies.
And you will cut off all them that afflict my soul,
for I am your servant.

PRAYER

God, who gave peace to humanity and the heavenly
choirs of angels through the Blood and Cross of our
Lord Jesus Christ, your Son: grant that we might be
filled with the abundance of your peace and rejoice
in unity with the choirs of angels. Through Christ
our Lord. Amen.

A MEDIEVAL LITTLE OFFICE OF
SAINT BENEDICT

The following office is one of the earliest to honor Saint Benedict. Monastics and oblates tend to look on Saint Benedict as a gracious and loving father and a heavenly intercessor. This set of prayers highlights important events in Saint Benedict's life as he responded to the world around him, calling to mind how he can serve as a model of discipleship in all times. This office can be said on Saint Benedict's feast days (March 21st and July 11th), on the anniversary of a monastic profession or oblation, or when one wants to feel closer to this fatherly holy man. Depending on whether you say the office or chant it, you might want to set aside around 8–10 minutes to pray this office.

Antiphon 1: Behold, the man of God, Benedict, left the world and followed the Lord.

PSALM 15

Lord, who shall dwell in your tent?
or who shall rest in your holy mountain?
He that walks without blemish

and that works justice.
He that speaks truth in his heart,
who has not used deceit in his tongue.
Nor has done evil to his neighbor,
nor taken up a reproach against his neighbors.
In his sight the malignant is brought to nothing,
but he glorifies them that fear the Lord.
He that swears to his neighbor and deceives not,
he that has not put out his money to usury
nor taken bribes against the innocent.
He that does these things
shall not be moved for ever.

Glory be to the Father and to the Son and to the
   Holy Spirit.
As it was in the beginning, is now, and ever shall
   be, world without end. Amen.

Antiphon 1: Behold, the man of God, Benedict, left
the world and followed the Lord.

Antiphon 2: Brother Maur, run quickly, for the boy
Placid has fallen into the current.

The earth is the Lord's and the fullness thereof,
the world and all they that dwell therein.
For he has founded it upon the seas
and has prepared it upon the rivers.
Who shall ascend into the mountain of the Lord,
or who shall stand in his holy place?
The innocent in hands and clean of heart,
who has not taken his soul in vain
nor sworn deceitfully to his neighbor.
He shall receive a blessing from the Lord,
and mercy from God his Savior.
This is the generation of them that seek him,
of them that seek the face of the God of Jacob.
Lift up your gates, O princes,
and be lifted up, O eternal gates,
and the King of Glory shall enter in.
Who is this King of Glory?
the Lord who is strong and mighty,
the Lord mighty in battle.
Lift up your gates, O princes,
and be lifted up, O eternal gates,
and the King of Glory shall enter in.
Who is this King of Glory?
the Lord of hosts, he is the King of Glory.

Glory be to the Father . . .

Antiphon 2: Brother Maur, run quickly, for the boy Placid has fallen into the current.

Antiphon 3: The Lord's power bestowed this great grace upon him: all the world was gathered up into one ray of sunlight in his sight.

PSALM 34

I will bless the Lord at all times;
his praise shall be always in my mouth.
In the Lord shall my soul be praised;
let the meek hear and rejoice.
O magnify the Lord with me,
and let us extol his name together.
I sought the Lord and he heard me,
and he delivered me from all my troubles.
Come to him and be enlightened,
and your faces shall not be confounded.
This poor man cried and the Lord heard him
and saved him out of all his troubles.
The angel of the Lord shall encamp
round about them that fear him
and shall deliver them.
O taste and see that the Lord is sweet;
blessed is the man that hopes in him.
Fear the Lord, all you his saints,
for there is no want to them that fear him.

The rich have wanted and have suffered hunger,
but they that seek the Lord shall not be deprived
of any good.
Come, children, hearken to me!
I will teach you the fear of the Lord.
Who is the man that desires life,
who loves to see good days?
Keep your tongue from evil
and your lips from speaking guile.
Turn away from evil and do good,
seek after peace and pursue it.
The eyes of the Lord are upon the just
and his ears unto their prayers.
But the countenance of the Lord
is against them that do evil things,
to cut off the remembrance of them from the earth.
The just cried, and the Lord heard them,
and delivered them out of all their troubles.
The Lord is near unto them that are of a contrite
heart,
and he will save the humble of spirit.
Many are the afflictions of the just,
but out of them all will the Lord deliver them.
The Lord keeps all their bones,
not one of them shall be broken.
The death of the wicked is very evil,

and they that hate the just shall be guilty.
The Lord will redeem the souls of his servants,
and none of them that trust in him shall offend.

Glory be to the Father . . .

Antiphon 3: The Lord's power bestowed this great grace upon him: all the world was gathered up into one ray of sunlight in his sight.

Versicle: And so, he left in learned ignorance.
Response: And wisely unlearned.

Our Father . . .

Absolution: May the all-powerful and merciful Lord absolve us from the imprisonment of our sins.
Response: Amen.

Reader's Petition [if a priest or bishop is present to respond:]
Father, give the blessing.

[or, if a priest or bishop is not present to respond, or if the reader is a bishop:] Lord, give a blessing.
Blessing
[said by a priest or bishop if present, omitted if not present:]
May the blessed confessor Benedict plead for us on account of our sins.

First Reading

There was a man of venerable life, "blessed" in grace and in name, who from his youth bore within himself the heart of maturity, since, surpassing his natural age in his manner of living, he never abandoned his heart to any frivolous pleasure. But you, O Lord, have mercy upon us.

Versicle: The young man of the Lord, Benedict, having abandoned his studies, longed for the desert. His nurse, who loved him dearly, alone went with him.

Response: And so, he left in learned ignorance and wisely unlearned. His nurse, who loved him dearly, alone went with him.

Second Reading

May we, who have come eagerly from every part of the earth to the teaching of the most blessed Benedict, learn to spurn what he spurned and esteem what he esteemed. For, if we wish to follow him to glory, we must imitate the way he left us. But you, O Lord, have mercy upon us.

Versicle: The servant of God Benedict preferred to endure the misfortunes of this world rather than its praises, to be wearied in labors for God rather than to be lifted up by the favors of this life.

Response: Fleeing his nurse in secret, he made for a secluded and deserted place, to be wearied in labors for God rather than to be lifted up by the favors of this life.

Third Reading

Most beloved, let us examine every aspect of our life, and let us remove every impurity, all ill will. Let us be gentle, moderate, and humble. Let us follow the virtues of peace and charity. Let us hold to our father's precepts and follow in his footsteps, so that together with him we might obtain eternal joy. But you, O Lord, have mercy upon us.

Versicle: In the middle of the night, blessed Benedict beheld a flowing light from above that drove away every shadow of night. In such splendor it illuminated everything, so that that light excelled daylight itself.

Response: As he himself reported to his disciples, he was taken up because all the world was gathered before the eyes of his soul in one ray of sunlight. In such splendor it illuminated everything. Glory be to the Father and to the Son and to the Holy Spirit. So that that light excelled daylight itself.

Hymn　　　　Te Decet Laus

It is right to praise you;
it is right to sing hymns to you.
Glory to you:
God the Father and the Son
with the Holy Spirit,
world without end. Amen.

Prayer

Help us, we pray, O Lord, to imitate here on earth
the works of our most blessed father Benedict, that
we might merit to share his glory there in heaven.
Through our Lord Jesus Christ, your Son, who lives
and reigns with you and the Holy Spirit, one God
for ever and ever.
Response: Amen.

Versicle: The Lord be with you.
Response: And with your spirit.

[The versicle and response immediately above are not said
when reciting alone or when the speaker of the versicle
has not been ordained a deacon. In this case, the following
versicle and response are said instead.]

Versicle: O Lord, hear my prayer.
Response: And let my cry come to you.

Versicle: Let us bless the Lord.
Response: Thanks be to God.

Versicle: May the souls of the faithful departed, through the mercy of God, rest in peace.
Response: Amen.

AN EARLY MODERN LITTLE OFFICE OF
SAINT BENEDICT

The following office was made during the turbulent time after the Reformation. After all the monasteries in England had been eliminated, some courageous men and women went to the Continent to remake the English Benedictine Congregation, and the compiler of this office was one of them. Even in the midst of very difficult times, offices such as this can provide structure and comfort. As noted in the introduction to the last office, monastics and oblates tend to look on Saint Benedict as a gracious and loving father and a heavenly intercessor. This set of prayers focuses on Saint Benedict's miracles and his power as an intercessor with God, reflecting the tough times these Benedictines were enduring. This early modern office might best be said when we are in greater need of consolation or are enduring difficult times of our own. Of course, it would be appropriate on Saint Benedict's feast days (March 21st and July 11th) or on the anniversary of a monastic profession or oblation as well. Since this office has all the different hours, you might want to set aside around 3–4 minutes to pray each of the Hours throughout the day, with additional time for silence if possible.

Versicle: O Lord, open my lips.
Response: And my mouth will declare your praise.

Versicle: O God, come to my assistance.
Response: O Lord, make haste to help me.

Glory be to the Father and to the Son and to the Holy Spirit.
As it was in the beginning, is now, and ever shall be, world without end. Amen.

Hymn
Aurora fair unmasks her face,
and smiles upon the earth to see,
Benedict's soul, adorned with grace,
ascend to heav'n so gloriously.

How gracious is he there above,
who here on earth did shine so bright,
whose wonders, stony hearts did move,
and gave to all the world his light?

Praise, honor, glory without end
to you, O sacred Trinity,
which Benedict your faithful friend
enjoys now for eternity. Amen.

Antiphon: There was a man of venerable life, blessed in grace and name, who even from his childhood, bearing a grave mind and transcending his age in virtuous conversation, gave his mind to no voluptuousness.

Versicle: Pray for us, O blessed Father Benedict.
Response: That we may be made worthy of the promises of Christ.

PRAYER

O God, who called the blessed father and lawmaker Saint Benedict from all worldly tumults to serve you alone, grant to all and especially those who serve under his discipline constant perseverance in virtue and perfect victory at their end. Through Jesus Christ, your Son, who lives and reigns with you, world without end. Amen.

Versicle: O God, come to my assistance.
Response: O Lord, make haste to help me.

Glory be to the Father . . .

Hymn
Great conductor in sacred war,
who never conquered was by might,
defend us with thy holy prayer
and strengthen us when we do fight.

Protect us from all sin's disgrace,
who made the blackbird to retire—
which flutt'ring came about your face
to tempt you with unchaste desire.

Praise, honor, glory without end
to you, O sacred Trinity,
which Benedict your faithful friend
enjoys now for eternity. Amen.

Antiphon: Our powerful Lord did so great a favor to blessed Benedict that under one sunbeam he saw the whole world.

Versicle: Pray for us, O blessed Father Benedict.
Response: That we may be made worthy of the promises of Christ.

PRAYER

Make us, we beseech you, O Lord, to imitate here the labors of the blessed father Saint Benedict, that there we may be partakers of his glory. Through Jesus Christ our Lord. Amen.

 TERCE

Versicle: O God, come to my assistance.
Response: O Lord, make haste to help me.

Glory be to the Father . . .

Hymn
To free yourself from base desire
your flesh the wounds of thorns endured,
and thus you put out fire with fire,
and one wound with another cured.

With sign of Cross a poisoned cup,
you broke in two with pow'r divine;
that poison you had drunken up,
but death was weaker than life's sign.

Praise, honor, glory without end
to you, O sacred Trinity,
which Benedict your faithful friend
enjoys now for eternity. Amen.

Antiphon: The man of our Lord, Benedict, was of a pleasant countenance, and adorned with angelic gray hair. And so great was the brightness that shone about him, that, being yet upon the earth, he seemed to dwell in heaven.

Versicle: Pray for us, O blessed Father Benedict.
Response: That we may be made worthy of the promises of Christ.

PRAYER

We beseech you, O Lord, that the intercession of the blessed abbot Saint Benedict may so recommend us, that what by our own merits we cannot obtain we may obtain by his patronage. Through Christ our Lord. Amen.

Versicle: O God, come to my assistance.
Response: O Lord, make haste to help me.

Glory be to the Father . . .

Hymn
A monk there was when others prayed,
oft pulled away from serving God,
who afterwards became most stayed,
when he was stricken with your rod.

The earth their bones did vomit out,
who did in your disfavor die.
But those to you that were devout
did walk upon the waters dry.

Praise, honor, glory without end
to you, O sacred Trinity,
which Benedict your faithful friend
enjoys now for eternity. Amen.

Antiphon: The glorious confessor of our Lord, Benedict, leading an angelic life upon earth, was made a mirror of good works to the world and so rejoices in heaven without end.

Versicle: Pray for us, O blessed Father Benedict.
Response: That we may be made worthy of the promises of Christ.

PRAYER

O God, in whose power holy Saint Benedict made the dead members of a child revive, grant, we beseech you, that for his merits we may by the breath of your Spirit be brought to life from the death of our souls. Through Christ our Lord. Amen.

——————— NONE ———————

Versicle: O God, come to my assistance.
Response: O Lord, make haste to help me.

Glory be to the Father . . .

Hymn

The compass of the world so round
he in a sunbeam did descry.
Nothing on earth so strange was found
that was concealed from his keen eye.

O holy Saint! O heav'nly man!
to whom God did his secrets tell,
who saw the soul of Saint German
ascend the heav'ns, for aye to dwell.

Praise, honor, glory without end
to you, O sacred Trinity,
which Benedict your faithful friend
enjoys now for eternity. Amen.

Antiphon: The man of God, Benedict, was
replenished with the spirit of all righteous men.
May he pray for all professors of the catholic faith.

Versicle: Pray for us, O blessed Father Benedict.
Response: That we may be made worthy of the
promises of Christ.

PRAYER

Grant us, we beseech you, O Lord, that with cheerful mind we may daily celebrate the memory of your blessed confessor Benedict, whose life, graced with many miracles, was well pleasing to you. Through Christ our Lord. Amen.

VESPERS

Versicle: O God, come to my assistance.
Response: O Lord, make haste to help me.

Glory be to the Father . . .

Hymn
His sister's soul, from sin most free,
and beautified with heav'nly love
flying to heaven's throne he sees
in likeness of a milk-white dove.

O blessèd saints of God beloved,
who lie entombed both in one grave:
one heart you had, while here you moved,
one glory now in heaven have.

Praise, honor, glory without end
to you, O sacred Trinity,
which Benedict your faithful friend
enjoys now for eternity. Amen.

Antiphon: Towards the east appeared a straight path, reaching from his cell even to heaven. And a man of venerable features, shining brightly and standing near it, demanded whose path that was. When they confessed they did not know, he said to them, "This is the path by which Benedict, beloved of our Lord, ascended to heaven."

Versicle: Pray for us, O blessed Father Benedict.
Response: That we may be made worthy of the promises of Christ.

Prayer

We beseech you, O almighty God, by the merits and prayers of the most blessed father Saint Benedict, of his disciples Saint Placid and Saint Maur, of the Virgin his sister Saint Scholastica, and of all holy monks and nuns who under his banner and conduct have fought for you: that you would renew in us your Holy Spirit, by whose inspiration we may make war against the flesh, the world, and the devil. And, because the palm of victory cannot be achieved without laborious battle, give us in adversity patience, in temptation constancy, in perils counsel. Give us the purity of chastity, the desire of poverty, the fruit of obedience, and a firm purpose to observe your commandments, so that being strengthened with your consolation and linked in brotherly charity, we may serve you with one heart and so pass over these temporal things that, being crowned for our victories, we may deserve at last in the company of those religious troops to attain those eternal good things. Through Christ our Lord. Amen.

COMPLINE

Versicle: Convert us, O Lord our Savior.
Response: And avert your wrath from us.

Versicle: O God, come to my assistance.
Response: O Lord, make haste to help me.

Glory be to the Father . . .

Hymn

Blesséd Patriarch we you pray,
and also crave in humble wise,
that unto heav'n you'd show the way
whom you the earth taught to despise.

Grant we may seek those joys above
and mend in us what is amiss,
that living here in Christian love,
we may hereafter live in bliss.

Praise, honor, glory without end
to you, O sacred Trinity,
which Benedict your faithful friend
enjoys now for eternity. Amen.

Antiphon: Let the whole company of all the faithful rejoice for the glory of the blessed abbot Saint Benedict. Let the troops of religious chiefly exult, celebrating his memory upon the earth for whose society the saints rejoice in heaven.

Versicle: Pray for us, O blessed Father Benedict.
Response: That we may be made worthy of the promises of Christ.

Prayer: Purify, O God, the hearts of all those who, forsaking worldly vanities, you have encouraged to aspire to the reward of a more perfect vocation, under the discipline of their holy patriarch and founder Saint Benedict. And pour your grace into them, whereby they may persevere in you, and by your assistance accomplish what by your inspiration they have promised, that so achieving the perfection which they possess, they may also merit to attain the reward you proposed to such as should persevere in you. Through our Lord Jesus Christ, who lives and reigns with you in the unity of the Holy Spirit. Amen.

THE LITTLE OFFICE OF
SAINT SCHOLASTICA[18]

The following office is said in honor of Saint Benedict's sister Saint Scholastica, the first Benedictine nun. As she is the special patron of all Benedictine nuns and sisters, this office is especially valuable for those who are women Benedictines or are associated with their monasteries. The hymns in this office describe the only event of Saint Scholastica's life we know clearly—when God sent a rainstorm to prevent Saint Benedict from leaving Saint Scholastica once she prayed for him to remain with her in talk through the night. This office can be said on Scholastica's feast day (February 10th), on the anniversary of a monastic profession or oblation, or when one wants to feel closer to this mother of Benedictines. Depending on whether you say the office or chant it, you might want to set aside around 2–3 minutes to pray this office, ideally making time for silence afterward.

18 This Little Office is printed in the prayer book for Benedictines and their associates compiled by Fr. Wendelin Maria Mayer, OSB. I have adapted the language at times for modern readers but not changed the office in substance. This text includes the Hour of Prime, which was suppressed at Vatican II. If one celebrates the Liturgy of the Hours according to the pre-Vatican II Roman Rite or another Latin Rite that recognizes Prime, feel free to use this Hour.

Versicle: O Lord, open my lips.
Response: And my mouth will declare your praise.

Versicle: O God, come to my assistance.
Response: O Lord, make haste to help me.

Glory be to the Father and to the Son and to the
Holy Spirit.
As it was in the beginning, is now, and ever shall
be, world without end. Amen.

Hymn
You, virgin, spouse of Christ, all hail!
while dwelling in this earthly vale
your love of Him did never fail,
bright burning to the last.

While songs of joy we raise to you,
we pray you, too, our souls make true,
from toils which Satan's ghastly crew
has wily round them cast.

To God the Father and the Son
and Holy Spirit, Three in One,
be honor, glory, fame, and praise,
for an eternal length of days. Amen.

Antiphon   WISDOM 4:1
Better is childlessness with virtue;
for immortal is the memory of virtue,
acknowledged both by God and human beings.

PRAYER
Mercifully look down upon your family, we beseech
you, O Lord, through the merits of your blessed
virgin, Saint Scholastica. And, as by her prayers
you caused the rain to descend from heaven,
grant through her supplications that the dryness
of our hearts might be moistened with the dew of
heavenly grace. Through Christ our Lord. Amen.

———— LAUDS ————

Versicle: O God, come to my assistance.
Response: O Lord, make haste to help me.

Glory be to the Father . . .

Hymn

Purest of doves, with brilliant eyes,
for Christ's dear sake you did despise
all joys and home with all its ties,
as naught you did esteem.

Oh, teach us then our souls to raise
to God on high in hymns of praise,
that we with him through endless days
may live in bliss supreme.

To God the Father and the Son
and Holy Spirit, Three in One,
be honor, glory, fame, and praise,
for an eternal length of days. Amen.

Antiphon   SONG OF SONGS 2:10

My lover speaks and says to me,
"Arise, my friend, my beautiful one,
and come!"

PRAYER

Mercifully look down upon your family, we beseech you, O Lord, through the merits of your blessed virgin, Saint Scholastica. And, as by her prayers you caused the rain to descend from heaven, grant through her supplications that the dryness

of our hearts might be moistened with the dew of
heavenly grace. Through Christ our Lord. Amen.

PRIME
(if celebrated)

Versicle: O God, come to my assistance.
Response: O Lord, make haste to help me.

Glory be to the Father . . .

Hymn
Your brother's spotless chastity,
his love of holy poverty,
the life he led so holily,
you strive now to surpass.

In him the glorious sun we see,
in you the shining moon's mild beam,
by whose refulgent brilliancy
we this world's darkness pass.

To God the Father and the Son
and Holy Spirit, Three in One,
be honor, glory, fame, and praise,
for an eternal length of days. Amen.

Antiphon   SONG OF SONGS 2:1–2

I am a flower of Sharon,
a lily of the valleys.

Like a lily among thorns,
so is my friend among women.

PRAYER

Mercifully look down upon your family, we beseech you, O Lord, through the merits of your blessed virgin, Saint Scholastica. And, as by her prayers you caused the rain to descend from heaven, grant through her supplications that the dryness of our hearts might be moistened with the dew of heavenly grace. Through Christ our Lord. Amen.

 TERCE

Versicle: O God, come to my assistance.
Response: O Lord, make haste to help me.

Glory be to the Father . . .

Hymn

Guided by love, each year your feet
sought your dear brother's blessed retreat,
there to enjoy in converse sweet
the words of life and light.

Blessed intercourse for God was there,
your tongues to guide, your words to hear,
and your devoted hearts to cheer
with goodness infinite.

To God the Father and the Son
and Holy Spirit, Three in One,
be honor, glory, fame, and praise,
for an eternal length of days. Amen.

Antiphon   SONG OF SONGS 8:7
Deep waters cannot quench love,
nor rivers sweep it away.

PRAYER

Mercifully look down upon your family, we beseech
you, O Lord, through the merits of your blessed
virgin, Saint Scholastica. And, as by her prayers
you caused the rain to descend from heaven,
grant through her supplications that the dryness
of our hearts might be moistened with the dew of
heavenly grace, through Christ our Lord. Amen.

Versicle: O God, come to my assistance.
Response: O Lord, make haste to help me.

Glory be to the Father . . .

Hymn
Your loving heart had more delight
to speak and meditate aright
of future life than in the sight
and taste of worldly joy.

And so earnestly you did pray,
your brother with you kind to stay,
and all the night till dawn of day
with pious words employ.

To God the Father and the Son
and Holy Spirit, Three in One,
be honor, glory, fame, and praise,
for an eternal length of days. Amen.

Antiphon   HOSEA 2:21–22

I will betroth you to me forever:

I will betroth you to me with justice and with judgment,

with loyalty and with compassion;

I will betroth you to me with fidelity,
and you shall know the LORD.

PRAYER

Mercifully look down upon your family, we beseech you, O Lord, through the merits of your blessed virgin, Saint Scholastica. And, as by her prayers you caused the rain to descend from heaven, grant through her supplications that the dryness of our hearts might be moistened with the dew of heavenly grace. Through Christ our Lord. Amen.

——— NONE ———

Versicle: O God, come to my assistance.
Response: O Lord, make haste to help me.

Glory be to the Father . . .

Hymn

When of your wish he took no heed,
with head inclined you did proceed
to pray to Christ in this your need,
and help you did obtain.

Till then the sky had been serene,
when suddenly dark clouds were seen
with thunder's roll and lightning's sheen
pouring torrents of rain.

To God the Father and the Son
and Holy Spirit, Three in One,
be honor, glory, fame, and praise,
for an eternal length of days. Amen.

Antiphon   Psalm 27:4

One thing I ask of the Lord;
this I seek:
To dwell in the Lord's house
all the days of my life,
To gaze on the Lord's beauty,
to visit his temple.

Prayer

Mercifully look down upon your family, we beseech
you, O Lord, through the merits of your blessed

virgin, Saint Scholastica. And, as by her prayers you caused the rain to descend from heaven, grant through her supplications that the dryness of our hearts might be moistened with the dew of heavenly grace, through Christ our Lord. Amen.

VESPERS

Versicle: O God, come to my assistance.
Response: O Lord, make haste to help me.

Glory be to the Father . . .

Hymn
So, forced by heav'n the brother stayed
and granted all for which she prayed,
and by his holy words allayed
her thirst for converse blessed.

To him at dawn she bade farewell,
deep in her heart his lessons dwell.
In three short days, death's parting knell
called her away to rest.

To God the Father and the Son
and Holy Spirit, Three in One,
be honor, glory, fame, and praise,
for an eternal length of days. Amen.

Antiphon　　　SIRACH 35:21–22
The prayer of the lowly pierces the clouds;
it does not rest till it reaches its goal;
Nor will it withdraw till the Most High responds,
judges justly and affirms the right.

PRAYER

Mercifully look down upon your family, we beseech you, O Lord, through the merits of your blessed virgin, Saint Scholastica. And, as by her prayers you caused the rain to descend from heaven, grant through her supplications that the dryness of our hearts might be moistened with the dew of heavenly grace. Through Christ our Lord. Amen.

Versicle: O God, come to my assistance.
Response: O Lord, make haste to help me.

Glory be to the Father . . .

Hymn
Her holy soul, like some pure dove,
has winged its way to heav'n above,
her body chaste is placed with love
within her brother's grave.

Blessed saint, consumed with love divine,
while heav'n's bright rays around you shine
and joys eternal you entwine,
our souls from danger save.

To God the Father and the Son
and Holy Spirit, Three in One,
be honor, glory, fame, and praise,
for an eternal length of days. Amen.

Antiphon SONG OF SONGS 2:10–11, 13
Arise, my friend, my beautiful one,
and come!

For see, the winter is past,
the rains are over and gone.

Arise, my friend, my beautiful one,
and come!

Versicle: Who will give me wings as a dove?
Response: And I will fly and be at rest.

PRAYER

Mercifully look down upon your family, we beseech you, O Lord, through the merits of your blessed virgin, Saint Scholastica. And, as by her prayers you caused the rain to descend from heaven, grant through her supplications that the dryness of our hearts might be moistened with the dew of heavenly grace. Through Christ our Lord. Amen.

THE LITTLE OFFICE OF
SAINT GERTRUDE
THE GREAT[19]

This simple and touching office is said in honor of the impressive medieval mystic Saint Gertrude the Great. Gertrude was an early female author, composing a number of works, and her visions were renowned. Her visions of the Sacred Heart in particular, influential throughout Europe, are reflected in the hymns given here. This office can be said on Saint Gertrude's feast day (November 16th) and would also be appropriate on the Solemnity of the Sacred Heart. Depending on whether you say the office or chant it, you might want to set aside around 2–3 minutes to pray this office, ideally making time for silence afterward.

19 This Little Office is printed in the prayer book for
    Benedictines and their associates compiled by Fr.
    Wendelin Maria Mayer, OSB. I have adapted the
    language at times for modern readers but not changed
    the office in substance. This text includes the office
    of Prime, which was suppressed at Vatican II. If one
    celebrates the Liturgy of the Hours according to the
    pre-Vatican II Roman Rite or another Latin Rite that
    recognizes Prime, feel free to use this Hour.

Versicle: O Lord, open my lips.
Response: And my mouth will declare your praise.

Versicle: O God, come to my assistance.
Response: O Lord, make haste to help me.

Glory be to the Father and to the Son and to the
    Holy Spirit.
As it was in the beginning, is now, and ever shall
    be, world without end. Amen.

Hymn
Dear Spouse of virgins, hear us sing
with joy a virgin's praise,
whom you did in your love prepare
to join angelic lays.

And hear us too, O Gertrude, now,
while we your joys proclaim,
chanting this office with sweet voice
in honor of your name.

Praise be to Father and to Son
and to the Paraclete,
by whom this spouse unto her Lord
was joined in union sweet.

Versicle: Pray for us, O holy virgin Gertrude.
Response: That we may be made worthy of the promises of Christ.

PRAYER

O God, who delighted to dwell in the most pure heart of the blessed Gertrude, purify our hearts by her merits and intercession, that they may become a habitation worthy of your divine Majesty, who lives and reigns with you in the unity of the Holy Spirit, world without end. Amen.

——————— LAUDS ———————

Versicle: O God, come to my assistance.
Response: O Lord, make haste to help me.

Glory be to the Father . . .

Hymn
Before all ages you were chos'n,
O Gertrude, to obtain
the richest treasures which the love
of Christ, your Spouse, can gain.

For this be praise to God on high
and unto Christ your love,
with holy and eternal laud
to God the Spir't above.

Versicle: Pray for us, O holy virgin Gertrude.
Response: That we may be made worthy of the promises of Christ.

PRAYER

O God, who delighted to dwell in the most pure heart of the blessed Gertrude, purify our hearts by her merits and intercession, that they may become a habitation worthy of your divine Majesty, who lives and reigns with you in the unity of the Holy Spirit, world without end. Amen.

——— PRIME ———
(If celebrated)

Versicle: O God, come to my assistance.
Response: O Lord, make haste to help me.

Glory be to the Father . . .

Hymn
Your early dawn of life was filled
with equal love and light,
which sweetly drew your heart and soul
to realms of pure delight.

For this be praise to God on high
and unto Christ your love,
with holy and eternal laud
to God the Spir't above.

Versicle: Pray for us, O holy virgin Gertrude.
Response: That we may be made worthy of the
promises of Christ.

Prayer

O God, who delighted to dwell in the most pure
heart of the blessed Gertrude, purify our hearts by
her merits and intercession, that they may become
a habitation worthy of your divine Majesty, who
lives and reigns with you in the unity of the Holy
Spirit, world without end. Amen.

Versicle: O God, come to my assistance.
Response: O Lord, make haste to help me.

Glory be to the Father . . .

Hymn
You have no other spouse but Christ,
to him your pure soul turns.
And every thought of other love,
for love of him it spurns.

For this be praise to God on high
and unto Christ your love,
with holy and eternal laud
to God the Spir't above.

Versicle: Pray for us, O holy virgin Gertrude.
Response: That we may be made worthy of the promises of Christ.

PRAYER

O God, who delighted to dwell in the most pure heart of the blessed Gertrude, purify our hearts by her merits and intercession, that they may become a habitation worthy of your divine Majesty, who lives and reigns with you in the unity of the Holy Spirit, world without end. Amen.

SEXT

Versicle: O God, come to my assistance.
Response: O Lord, make haste to help me.

Glory be to the Father . . .

Hymn
Your spouse within your heart enthroned
keeps regal state and finds his rest,
while others scorn his gentle rule,
or drive away the heav'nly Guest.

For this be praise to God on high
and unto Christ your love,
with holy and eternal laud
to God the Spir't above.

Versicle: Pray for us, O holy virgin Gertrude.
Response: That we may be made worthy of the promises of Christ.

Prayer

O God, who delighted to dwell in the most pure heart of the blessed Gertrude, purify our hearts by her merits and intercession, that they may become a habitation worthy of your divine Majesty, who lives and reigns with you in the unity of the Holy Spirit, world without end. Amen.

 NONE

Versicle: O God, come to my assistance.
Response: O Lord, make haste to help me.

Glory be to the Father . . .

Hymn
Stronger than death is that strong love
that burns within your virgin breast,
mourning your Jesus slain for you,
in whom alone your heart can rest.

For this be praise to God on high
and unto Christ your love,
with holy and eternal laud
to God the Spir't above.

Versicle: Pray for us, O holy virgin Gertrude.
Response: That we may be made worthy of the promises of Christ.

PRAYER

O God, who delighted to dwell in the most pure heart of the blessed Gertrude, purify our hearts by her merits and intercession, that they may become a habitation worthy of your divine Majesty, who lives and reigns with you in the unity of the Holy Spirit, world without end. Amen.

VESPERS

Versicle: O God, come to my assistance.
Response: O Lord, make haste to help me.

Glory be to the Father . . .

Hymn

With the right hand of love he wounds,
with the right hand he vict'ry gains
for love's own victim, who with him
in everlasting triumph reigns.

For this be praise to God on high
and unto Christ your love,
with holy and eternal laud
to God the Spir't above.

Versicle: Pray for us, O holy virgin Gertrude.
Response: That we may be made worthy of the
promises of Christ.

PRAYER

O God, who delighted to dwell in the most pure
heart of the blessed Gertrude, purify our hearts by
her merits and intercession, that they may become
a habitation worthy of your divine Majesty, who
lives and reigns with you in the unity of the Holy
Spirit, world without end. Amen.

Versicle: O God, come to my assistance.
Response: O Lord, make haste to help me.

Glory be to the Father . . .

Hymn
And now your earthly race is o'er;
the conqu'ror's crown and palm is won,
and you will rest for evermore,
upon the Heart of God's dear Son.

For this be praise to God on high
and unto Christ your love,
with holy and eternal laud
to God the Spir't above.

Versicle: Pray for us, O holy virgin Gertrude.
Response: That we may be made worthy of the promises of Christ.

PRAYER

O God, who delighted to dwell in the most pure heart of the blessed Gertrude, purify our hearts by her merits and intercession, that they may become a habitation worthy of your divine Majesty, who lives and reigns with you in the unity of the Holy Spirit, world without end. Amen.

COMMEMORATIONS
TO BE SAID AFTER
THE DIVINE OFFICE

The Commemorations presented here are for either those who want to extend their celebration of the Liturgy of the Hours or those who do not pray the Liturgy of the Hours but wish to sanctify the morning and evening in a way that echoes the Hours. These could be a daily offering; or they could serve as an extra offering during a liturgical season such as Lent, Advent, or Easter; or a specific Commemoration might be offered on its own. For example, the Commemoration of the Trinity might be said on Trinity Sunday, or the Commemoration of Our Lady on her feast days, etc. If they are said straight through, plan to set aside 3–4 minutes for the whole series of morning and evening Commemorations. If silent meditation will be a more integral part of the celebration, 5–10 minutes might be more appropriate.

COMMEMORATIONS
TO BE SAID AFTER LAUDS
or
IN THE MORNING

COMMEMORATION OF THE TRINITY

Antiphon: We call upon you, we adore you, we praise you, O blessed Trinity.

Versicle: Let us bless the Father and the Son with the Holy Spirit, let us praise and exalt him forever. Blessed are you, O Lord, in the firmament of heaven, praiseworthy and glorious forever.
Response: May the name of the Lord be blessed, now and forever.

Prayer: Almighty and eternal God, who have permitted to your servants by the confession of true faith to acknowledge the glory of the eternal Trinity and, in the power of its majesty, to adore the Unity: we beseech you that, through the firmness of this faith, we might ever be defended from all adversities, you who live and reign forever. Amen.

VENERATION OF THE CROSS

Antiphon: Through the sign of the Cross, free us from our enemies, O God.

Versicle: Proclaim to the nations.
Response: For the Lord has ruled from the wood.

PRAYER

Be present with us, Lord our God, and defend those whom you make to rejoice in the honor of the holy Cross by its continual help. Through Christ our Lord. Amen.

COMMEMORATION OF OUR LADY

Antiphon: Blessed Mother and unmarried Virgin, glorious Queen of the world, intercede for us with the Lord.

Versicle: After childbirth you remained a Virgin; Mother of God, intercede for us.
Response: You are beautiful and charming in your delights, holy Mother of God.

PRAYER

Grant to us your servants, God, we beseech you, that we might enjoy perpetual health of mind and body and that we might be freed from present sadness and come to the happiness of future joys. Through the same Christ our Lord. Amen.

COMMEMORATION OF THE APOSTLES

Antiphon: Pray for us, holy apostles of God—Peter and Paul, true lights of the world.

Versicle: Their voice has gone out to all lands.
Response: Their words to the ends of the world.

PRAYER

We beseech you, all powerful God, that your blessed apostles Peter and Paul would implore your aid upon us, that, loosed from all our sins, we might be rescued from every danger. Through Christ our Lord. Amen.

COMMEMORATION OF SAINT BENEDICT

Antiphon: The man of the Lord, Benedict, was filled with the spirit of all the just; may he intercede for all who have professed the monastic life.

Versicle: The mouth of the just meditates on wisdom, and his tongue speaks judgment.
Response: The Law of God is in his heart.

PRAYER

Commend us Lord, we beseech you, to the intercession of your abbot blessed Benedict, that what we cannot obtain by our merits we might achieve through his patronage. Through Christ our Lord. Amen.

COMMEMORATION FOR PEACE

Antiphon: Give peace in our days, Lord, for there is no one else who does battle for us but you, our God.

Versicle: Let peace be in your strength.
Response: And abundance in your towers.

PRAYER

God, from whom all holy desires, proper counsel, and just works come: give to your servants that peace the world cannot give, that our hearts might be ready to obey your commandments and, lifted above the fear of our enemies, our time here might be under your protection in quiet. Through Christ our Lord. Amen.

COMMEMORATION OF ALL SAINTS

Antiphon: The saints will exult in glory and rejoice on their beds.

Versicle: Rejoice and exult in the Lord, you just.
Response: And glory, all you upright of heart.

PRAYER

We beseech you, Lord, through the intercession of all your saints, be well-pleased, grant us your favor, and give us the everlasting remedy for our ills. Through Christ our Lord. Amen.

COMMEMORATIONS
TO BE SAID AFTER VESPERS
or
IN THE EVENING

COMMEMORATION OF THE TRINITY

Antiphon: Free us, save us, justify us, O blessed Trinity.

Versicle: Let us bless the Father and the Son with the Holy Spirit, let us praise and exalt him forever. Blessed are you, O Lord, in the firmament of heaven, praiseworthy and glorious forever.
Response: May the name of the Lord be blessed, now and forever.

PRAYER

Almighty and eternal God, who have permitted to your servants by the confession of true faith to acknowledge the glory of the eternal Trinity and, in the power of its majesty, to adore the Unity: we beseech you that, through the firmness of this faith, we might ever be defended from all adversities, you who live and reign forever. Amen.

VENERATION OF THE CROSS

Antiphon: Save us, Christ our Savior, through the power of your Cross; you who saved Peter on the sea, have mercy on us.

Versicle: Proclaim to the nations.
Response: For the Lord has ruled from the wood.

PRAYER
Be present with us, Lord our God, and defend those whom you make to rejoice in the honor of the holy Cross by its continual help. Through Christ our Lord. Amen.

COMMEMORATION OF OUR LADY

Antiphon: Holy Mother of God, ever Virgin Mary, intercede for us with the Lord our God.

Versicle: After childbirth you remained a Virgin; Mother of God, intercede for us.
Response: You are beautiful and charming in your delights, holy Mother of God.

Grant to us your servants, God, we beseech you, that we might enjoy perpetual health of mind and body, and that we might be freed from present sadness and come to the happiness of future joys. Through the same Christ our Lord. Amen.

COMMEMORATION OF THE APOSTLES

Antiphon: Peter, apostle, and Paul, teacher of the Gentiles: let them teach us your Law, O Lord.

Versicle: Their voice has gone out to all lands.
Response: Their words to the ends of the world.

PRAYER

We beseech you, all powerful God, that your blessed apostles Peter and Paul would implore your aid upon us, that loosed from all our sins we might be rescued from every danger. Through Christ our Lord. Amen.

COMMEMORATION OF SAINT BENEDICT

Antiphon: The man of the Lord, Benedict, was filled with the spirit of all the just; may he intercede for all who have professed the monastic life.

Versicle: The mouth of the just meditates on wisdom and his tongue speaks judgment.
Response: The Law of God is in his heart.

PRAYER

Commend us Lord, we beseech you, to the intercession of your abbot blessed Benedict, that what we cannot obtain by our merits we might achieve through his patronage. Through Christ our Lord. Amen.

COMMEMORATION FOR PEACE

Antiphon: Give peace in our days, Lord, for there is no one else who does battle for us but you, our God.

Versicle: Let peace be in your strength.
Response: And abundance in your towers.

God, from whom all holy desires, proper counsel, and just works come, give to your servants that peace that the world cannot give, that our hearts might be ready to obey your commandments and, lifted above the fear of our enemies, our time here might be under your protection in quiet. Through Christ our Lord. Amen.

COMMEMORATION OF ALL SAINTS

Antiphon: O how glorious is the kingdom in which all the saints rejoice with Christ; clothed with white robes they follow the Lamb wherever he goes.

Versicle: Rejoice and exult in the Lord, you just.
Response: And glory, all you upright of heart.

PRAYER

We beseech you, Lord, to look mercifully upon our infirmity, and turn away from us every punishment that we have justly merited, through the intercession of all your saints. Through Christ our Lord. Amen.

BENEDICTINE
LITANIES

The Litanies in this section may be said at any time, but they might be most meaningful on the particular saint's feast day or if a particular intention is being prayed for. They can be said once or several days in a row (a "novena" of nine days would be a traditional number). They can be said/prayed alone, or if you have more than one person, they can be said or sung as a call and response. For call and response, one person says/sings the invocation while the other(s) sing(s) the repeated refrains in italics. Plan to set aside around 3–5 minutes, depending on whether you sing or say these litanies.

LITANY OF SAINT BENEDICT

(Feast Days: March 21st and July 11th)

Lord, have mercy.
Lord, have mercy.
Christ, have mercy.
Christ, have mercy.
Lord, have mercy.
Lord, have mercy.

Christ, hear us.
Christ, graciously hear us.

God, the Father of heaven, *have mercy on us.*
God, the Son, Redeemer of the world, *have mercy on us.*
God, the Holy Spirit, *have mercy on us.*
Holy Trinity, one God, *have mercy on us.*

Holy Mary, *pray for us.*
Holy Mother of God, *pray for us.*
Holy Virgin of virgins, *pray for us.*

Holy Father Saint Benedict, *pray for us.*
Father, worthy of admiration, *pray for us.*
Father, worthy of veneration, *pray for us.*

Father, worthy of love, *pray for us.*

Saint Benedict, who were gifted with sanctity from your childhood, *pray for us.*

Saint Benedict, who fled from the corrupt ways of vice, *pray for us.*

Saint Benedict, who loved a hermit's life, *pray for us.*

Saint Benedict, who were fed by Saint Romanus, *pray for us.*

Saint Benedict, who rolled yourself among the briars, *pray for us.*

Saint Benedict, conqueror of lust, *pray for us.*

Saint Benedict, teacher of rustics, *pray for us.*

Saint Benedict, restorer of the apostolic life, *pray for us.*

Saint Benedict, founder of monasteries, *pray for us.*

Saint Benedict, framer of rules, *pray for us.*

Saint Benedict, gentle teacher of monks, *pray for us.*

Saint Benedict, faithful observer of the precepts, *pray for us.*

Saint Benedict, most prudent guide of the erring, *pray for us.*

Saint Benedict, who divested death of its terrors, *pray for us.*

Saint Benedict, spurner of demons, *pray for us.*

Saint Benedict, destroyer of enchantments, *pray for us.*

Saint Benedict, foreknower of future events, *pray for us.*

Saint Benedict, who caused Saint Maur to walk upon the waters, *pray for us.*

Saint Benedict, who freed Saint Placid from the deep, *pray for us.*

Saint Benedict, who saw the soul of your sister ascending into heaven, *pray for us.*

Saint Benedict, who fortified yourself at your departure by receiving the Body and Blood of our Lord, *pray for us.*

Saint Benedict, who with your eyes raised to heaven breathed forth your spirit in the arms of your disciples, *pray for us.*

Saint Benedict, who by the straight path of the East ascended from your cell into heaven, *pray for us.*

Saint Benedict, who triumphantly entered heaven, *pray for us.*

Saint Benedict, who are now enjoying Christ in the embraces of eternal love, *pray for us.*

Lamb of God, who take away the sins of the world, *spare us, O Lord.*

Lamb of God, who take away the sins of the world, *graciously hear us, O Lord.*

Lamb of God, who take away the sins of the world, *have mercy on us.*

Versicle: Intercede for us, O holy Father Saint Benedict.

Response: That we may be made worthy of the promises of Christ.

Let us pray: Vouchsafe, O Lord, to defend from the snares of the devil, through the merits of your confessor our holy Father Saint Benedict, those whom you have been pleased to instruct by his teaching. Through Christ our Lord. Amen.

LITANY OF SAINT SCHOLASTICA

(Feast Day: February 10th)

Lord, have mercy.
Lord, have mercy.
Christ, have mercy.
Christ, have mercy.
Lord, have mercy.
Lord, have mercy.

Christ, hear us.
Christ, graciously hear us.

God, the Father of heaven, *have mercy on us.*
God, the Son, Redeemer of the world, *have mercy on us.*
God, the Holy Spirit, *have mercy on us.*
Holy Trinity, one God, *have mercy on us.*

Holy Mary, *pray for us.*
Holy Mother of God, *pray for us.*
Holy Virgin of virgins, *pray for us.*

Saint Scholastica, *pray for us.*
Saint Scholastica, true sister of Saint Benedict, *pray for us.*

Saint Scholastica, chosen by God from eternity, *pray for us.*

Saint Scholastica, predisposed to a holy life by the grace of Christ our Lord, *pray for us.*

Saint Scholastica, consecrated to God from your infancy, *pray for us.*

Saint Scholastica, always a virgin incorrupt, *pray for us.*

Saint Scholastica, espoused to Jesus Christ, *pray for us.*

Saint Scholastica, scholar of the Holy Spirit, *pray for us.*

Saint Scholastica, mirror of innocence, *pray for us.*

Saint Scholastica, model of perfection, *pray for us.*

Saint Scholastica, pattern of virtues, *pray for us.*

Saint Scholastica, glory of the monastic life, *pray for us.*

Saint Scholastica, mother of numberless virgins, *pray for us.*

Saint Scholastica, imitator of the angelic life, *pray for us.*

Saint Scholastica, full of faith in God, *pray for us.*

Saint Scholastica, replenished with hope of the goods of heaven, *pray for us.*

Saint Scholastica, ever burning with the love of the Spouse, *pray for us.*

Saint Scholastica, resplendent with humility, *pray for us.*

Saint Scholastica, trusting as a daughter in the Lord, *pray for us.*

Saint Scholastica, intent on prayer, *pray for us.*

Saint Scholastica, quickly heard by the Lord, *pray for us.*

Saint Scholastica, famed for the praise of perseverance, *pray for us.*

Saint Scholastica, who entered the courts of heaven in the shape of a dove, *pray for us.*

Saint Scholastica, who now follow the Lamb wheresoever he goes, *pray for us.*

Saint Scholastica, who rejoice in the delights of the Spouse forever, *pray for us.*

Saint Scholastica, adorned with a crown of glory, *pray for us.*

Saint Scholastica, advocate with God of those who invoke you, *pray for us.*

Saint Scholastica, generous patron of those who imitate you, *pray for us.*

Saint Scholastica, holy and innocent virgin, *pray for us.*

We, sinners, *beseech you to hear us.*

That you deign to help us by your most holy and efficacious prayers to God, *we beseech you to hear us.*

That you deign to cherish and preserve by your protection this monastery [or: home] and all who dwell therein, *we beseech you to hear us.*

That you deign to admit us into the number of your children, *we beseech you to hear us.*

That you deign to raise up, increase, and preserve our devotion to you, *we beseech you to hear us.*

That you deign to preserve in us the perfect observance of the Rule of your blessed brother, our most holy Father Saint Benedict, *we beseech you to hear us.*

That you deign by your supplications to moisten the dryness of our hearts with the dew of heavenly grace, *we beseech you to hear us.*

That by your intercession you might eternally unite us to Christ, the Spouse of our souls, *we beseech you to hear us.*

That you might lead us to eternal joys and to Jesus, our most sweet Spouse, *we beseech you to hear us.*

That you vouchsafe to hear us, *we beseech you to hear us.*

Lamb of God, who take away the sins of the world, *spare us, O Lord.*

Lamb of God, who take away the sins of the world, *graciously hear us, O Lord.*

Lamb of God, who take away the sins of the world, *have mercy on us.*

Versicle: Pray for us, O holy virgin Scholastica.

Response: That we may be made worthy of the promises of Christ.

Let us pray: O God, who to show the innocence of her life caused the soul of your blessed Virgin Scholastica to ascend into heaven in the form of a dove, grant by her merits and prayers that we might live so innocently as to deserve to arrive at eternal joys. Through Christ our Lord. Amen.

LITANY OF SAINT GERTRUDE THE GREAT

(Feast Day: November 16th)

Lord, have mercy.
Lord, have mercy.
Christ, have mercy.
Christ, have mercy.
Lord, have mercy.
Lord, have mercy.

Christ, hear us.
Christ, graciously hear us.

God, the Father of heaven, *have mercy on us.*
God, the Son, Redeemer of the world, *have mercy on us.*
God, the Holy Spirit, *have mercy on us.*
Holy Trinity, one God, *have mercy on us.*

Holy Mary, *pray for us.*

All you choirs of holy angels, *pray for us.*
All you saints and elect of God, *pray for us.*
Saint Gertrude, *pray for us.*
You chaste virgin, *pray for us.*
You beloved daughter of the heavenly Father, *pray for us.*

You chosen bride of Jesus Christ, *pray for us.*

You temple of the Holy Spirit, *pray for us.*

You joy of the Holy Trinity, *pray for us.*

You fragrant flower in the hand of Jesus Christ, *pray for us.*

You ever-blooming spring flower, *pray for us.*

You rose without thorns, *pray for us.*

You chaste dove without the stain of sin, *pray for us.*

You earthly seraph, *pray for us.*

You living sanctuary, *pray for us.*

You strong protection of all who venerate you, *pray for us.*

Jesus Christ, Spouse of Saint Gertrude, *have mercy on us.*

Through her humility, *have mercy on us.*

Through her charity, *have mercy on us.*

Through her untiring patience, *have mercy on us.*

Through the ardent love she bore you, *have mercy on us.*

Through the delight with which you dwelt in her heart, *have mercy on us.*

Through the love you have for her, *have mercy on us.*

Through the love with which you chose her from eternity, *have mercy on us.*

Through the love with which you so sweetly attracted her to yourself, *have mercy on us.*

Through the love with which you so delightfully united her to yourself, *have mercy on us.*

Through the love with which you so contentedly dwelt in her heart, *have mercy on us.*

Through the love with which you ended her life with a happy death, *have mercy on us.*

Through the love with which you conferred on her eternal life, *have mercy on us.*

Through the love with which you love and make joyful all the blessed, *have mercy on us.*

Jesus Christ, *have mercy on us.*

Lamb of God, who take away the sins of the world, *spare us, O Lord.*

Lamb of God, who take away the sins of the world, *graciously hear us, O Lord.*

Lamb of God, who take away the sins of the world, *have mercy on us.*

Let us pray: O holy virgin, Saint Gertrude, I beseech you, let me have a share in your great merits and intercession. Deign to look at the true love and great confidence I have in you. Write my name in your heart, and number me among those who enjoy your special care and protection, that through your merits my life may become well pleasing to God. Through Christ our Lord. Amen.

Versicle: Pray for us, O holy virgin Saint Gertrude.
Response: That we may be made worthy of the promises of Christ.

O Lord Jesus, by the love you bore to the virginal heart of Saint Gertrude, and by which you promised her that no sinner who would honor and love her should die a sudden and unprovided death, grant me, I beseech you, this grace, and let me so love you and repent of my sins, that with faith and confidence I may expect a happy death.

LITANY OF SAINT MAUR

Lord, have mercy.
Lord, have mercy.
Christ, have mercy.
Christ, have mercy.
Lord, have mercy.
Lord, have mercy.

Christ, hear us.
Christ, graciously hear us.

God, the Father of heaven, *have mercy on us.*
God, the Son, Redeemer of the world, *have mercy on us.*
God, the Holy Spirit, *have mercy on us.*
Holy Trinity, one God, *have mercy on us.*

Holy Mary, *pray for us.*
Holy Mother of God, *pray for us.*
Holy Virgin of virgins, *pray for us.*

Holy Abbot Saint Maur, *pray for us.*
Saint Maur, first disciple of Saint Benedict, *pray for us.*

Saint Maur, who from the first dawn of reason served God, *pray for us.*

Saint Maur, who from earliest youth despised the vanity of the world, *pray for us.*

Saint Maur, who while yet a child was placed under the care of Saint Benedict, *pray for us.*

Saint Maur, who by your advance in virtue gained the particular love of Saint Benedict, *pray for us.*

Saint Maur, who was regarded as a model of the monastic life, *pray for us.*

Saint Maur, illustrious for obedience, *pray for us.*

Saint Maur, who walked on the water as on solid ground to rescue Placid from the wave, *pray for us.*

Saint Maur, great lover of fasting, *pray for us.*

Saint Maur, who in a vision perceived the soul of Saint Benedict on a path of light ascend to heaven, *pray for us.*

Saint Maur, who for forty years governed your monasteries in great sanctity and finally yielded up your soul into the hands of your Creator, *pray for us.*

Saint Maur, great patron of all who invoke you, *pray for us.*

That we might follow your example, *pray for us.*

That we might be converted to God, *pray for us.*

That we might know the vanity of the world and fly from all danger of sin, *pray for us.*

That by keeping the commandments of God and his holy Church we might daily increase in virtue, *pray for us.*

That we might give a good example to our neighbor, *pray for us.*

That we might be obedient to our superiors, *pray for us.*

That we might despise all earthly good and practice self-denial, *pray for us.*

That we might, through charity, love and assist our neighbor, *pray for us.*

That we might love fasting, *pray for us.*

That freed from all sloth we might zealously strive to fulfill the will of God, *pray for us.*

That we might obtain the spirit of true devotion, *pray for us.*

That we might gain the grace of a happy death, *pray for us.*

That with you we might love and praise God eternally, *pray for us.*

Lamb of God, who take away the sins of the world, *spare us, O Lord.*

Lamb of God, who take away the sins of the world, *graciously hear us, O Lord.*

Lamb of God, who take away the sins of the world, *have mercy on us.*

Versicle: Pray for us, O holy Abbot Saint Maur.

Response: That we may be made worthy of the promises of Christ.

Let us pray: O God, who through the holy Abbot Saint Maur spread the Order of Saint Benedict throughout France, and there increased and preserved it, grant us in your mercy the grace that through the merits and intercession of this your faithful servant and all the holy sons of Saint Benedict, the Order may also be spread in our days, and that we might imitate the virtues of Saint Maur in such a manner as to gain heaven, where in company with the blessed, we may praise you for all eternity. Amen.

LITANY OF SAINT BERNARD

Lord, have mercy.
Lord, have mercy.
Christ, have mercy.
Christ, have mercy.
Lord, have mercy.
Lord, have mercy.

Christ, hear us.
Christ, graciously hear us.

God, the Father of heaven, *have mercy on us.*
God, the Son, Redeemer of the world, *have mercy on us.*
God, the Holy Spirit, *have mercy on us.*
Holy Trinity, one God, *have mercy on us.*

Holy Mary, Mother of God, *pray for us.*
Queen conceived without sin, *pray for us.*

Saint Bernard, *pray for us.*
Saint Bernard, who in giving yourself to God drew many souls to him, *pray for us.*
Saint Bernard, prodigy of the eleventh age, *pray for us.*

Saint Bernard, ornament of the clergy, *pray for us.*

Saint Bernard, terror of heretics, *pray for us.*

Saint Bernard, oracle of the Church, *pray for us.*

Saint Bernard, light of bishops, *pray for us.*

Saint Bernard, most humble, *pray for us.*

Saint Bernard, burning with zeal for the glory of God, *pray for us.*

Saint Bernard, most ardent for the honor of Mary, *pray for us.*

Saint Bernard, most beloved son of the Queen of angels, *pray for us.*

Saint Bernard, most pure in body and mind, *pray for us.*

Saint Bernard, perfect model of poverty and mortification, *pray for us.*

Saint Bernard, most ardent in charity to all, *pray for us.*

Saint Bernard, who feared God and not earthly powers, *pray for us.*

Saint Bernard, whose whole exterior breathed holiness, *pray for us.*

Saint Bernard, whose very look spoke of God, *pray for us.*

Saint Bernard, flower of religious, *pray for us.*

Saint Bernard, angel of Clairvaux, *pray for us.*

Saint Bernard, always absorbed in God, *pray for us.*

Lamb of God, who take away the sins of the world,
spare us, O Lord.
Lamb of God, who take away the sins of the world,
graciously hear us, O Lord.
Lamb of God, who take away the sins of the world,
have mercy on us.

Let us pray: O great saint, who from the very dawn of life turned all the powers of your soul and the noble affections of your pure and loving heart towards the Creator, angel clothed in mortal flesh, who appeared in this valley of tears as a bright lily of purity to shed around yourself the good odor of Christ to show to all the beauty of virtue and point out to thousands the way to heaven, O pray for us, that truly despising all earthly objects we might live to God alone. Amen.

LITANY OF ALL SAINTS OF
THE ORDER OF SAINT BENEDICT

(Feast Day: November 13th)

Lord, have mercy.
Lord, have mercy.
Christ, have mercy.
Christ, have mercy.
Lord, have mercy.
Lord, have mercy.

Christ, hear us.
Christ, graciously hear us.

God, the Father of heaven, *have mercy on us.*
God, the Son, Redeemer of the world, *have mercy on us.*
God, the Holy Spirit, *have mercy on us.*
Holy Trinity, one God, *have mercy on us.*

Holy Mary, *pray for us.*
Holy Mother of God, *pray for us.*
Holy Virgin of virgins, *pray for us.*

Holy Father Saint Benedict, *pray for us.*
Saint Benedict, gem of abbots, *pray for us.*

Saint Benedict, patriarch of monks, *pray for us.*
Saint Benedict, father of countless saints, *pray for us.*
Saint Placid, *pray for us.*
Saint Ewald, *pray for us.*
Saint Boniface, *pray for us.*
Saint Lambert, *pray for us.*
Saint Adalbert, *pray for us.*
Saint Meinrad, *pray for us.*
All you holy martyrs of our Order, *pray for us.*
Saint Gregory, *pray for us.*
Saint Peter Celestine, *pray for us.*
Saint Swithbert, *pray for us.*
Saint Willibrord, *pray for us.*
Saint Amandus, *pray for us.*
Saint Wulstan, *pray for us.*
Saint Leander, *pray for us.*
Saint Augustine of Canterbury, *pray for us.*
Saint Isidore, *pray for us.*
Saint Dunstan, *pray for us.*
Saint Æthelwold, *pray for us.*
Saint Ildephonse, *pray for us.*
Saint Anselm, *pray for us.*
Saint Willibald, *pray for us.*
Saint Gothhard, *pray for us.*
Saint Ansgar, *pray for us.*
Saint Ludger, *pray for us.*

Saint Benno, *pray for us.*

All you holy bishops of our Order, *pray for us.*

Saint Maur, *pray for us.*

Saint Othmar, *pray for us.*

Saint Bernard, *pray for us.*

Saint Robert, *pray for us.*

Saint Winnibald, *pray for us.*

Saint John Gualbert, *pray for us.*

Saint Sylvester, *pray for us.*

Saint Odo, *pray for us.*

Saint Odilo, *pray for us.*

Saint Majolus, *pray for us.*

Saint Bede, *pray for us.*

Saint Romuald, *pray for us.*

All you holy abbots and prelates of our Order, *pray for us.*

All you holy monks and hermits, *pray for us.*

Saint Scholastica, *pray for us.*

Saint Gertrude, *pray for us.*

Saint Hildegard, *pray for us.*

Saint Mechthild, *pray for us.*

Saint Lioba, *pray for us.*

Saint Thecla, *pray for us.*

Saint Elizabeth, *pray for us.*

Saint Lutgard, *pray for us.*

Saint Walburga, *pray for us.*

Saint Cunegonde, *pray for us.*
Saint Columba, *pray for us.*
Saint Frances, *pray for us.*
Saint Richarda, *pray for us.*
Saint Bathlida, *pray for us.*
Saint Etheldreda, *pray for us.*
Saint Editha, *pray for us.*
Saint Ethelburga, *pray for us.*
Saint Hilda, *pray for us.*
Saint Florintina, *pray for us.*
Saint Ebba and companions, *pray for us.*
All you holy virgins of our Order, *pray for us.*
All you holy empresses and queens, *pray for us.*

Be merciful to us. *Spare us, O Lord.*
Be merciful to us. *Graciously hear us, O Lord.*

From the temptations and snares of the devil,
   deliver us, O Lord.
From the concupiscence of the flesh, *deliver us, O
   Lord.*
From the concupiscence of the eyes, *deliver us, O
   Lord.*
From the pride of life, *deliver us, O Lord.*
From blindness of heart, *deliver us, O Lord.*
From all envy and hatred, *deliver us, O Lord.*

From all sloth and inordinate sadness, *deliver us, O Lord.*

From all anger and ill-will, *deliver us, O Lord.*

From all impatience and faintheartedness, *deliver us, O Lord.*

From the transgression of our vows, *deliver us, O Lord.*

From all occasions of sin, *deliver us, O Lord.*

From all sudden and unprovided death, *deliver us, O Lord.*

From the everlasting curse, *deliver us, O Lord.*

By your eternal generation from the Father, *deliver us, O Lord.*

By your nativity in time from your holy Mother, *deliver us, O Lord.*

By your most holy life and conversation, *deliver us, O Lord.*

By your most bitter Passion and death, *deliver us, O Lord.*

By your glorious Resurrection and Ascension, *deliver us, O Lord.*

By your coming to Judgment, *deliver us, O Lord.*

By the merits and intercessions of your saints, *deliver us, O Lord.*

We sinners, *we beseech you to hear us.*

That before all things, we might seek the kingdom of God and his justice, *we beseech you to hear us.*

That we might learn from you to be meek and humble of heart, *we beseech you to hear us.*

That we might deny ourselves, take up our cross, and follow you, *we beseech you to hear us.*

That we might willingly and eagerly take upon ourselves your sweet yoke and light burden, *we beseech you to hear us.*

That we might be careful to preserve the unity of the spirit in the bond of peace, *we beseech you to hear us.*

That walking in the spirit we might not accomplish the desires of the flesh, *we beseech you to hear us.*

That you might vouchsafe to raise up and to cherish in us the spirit of poverty, *we beseech you to hear us.*

That you might vouchsafe to give us compunction of heart and the gift of tears, *we beseech you to hear us.*

That you might vouchsafe to grant us the perfect mortification of our senses and of our own will, *we beseech you to hear us.*

That you might vouchsafe to persevere in your holy service our abbots, abbesses, superiors, and all the communities entrusted to them, *we beseech you to hear us.*

That you might vouchsafe to grant eternal rest to the souls of our brethren and benefactors, *we beseech you to hear us.*

That you might grant us to persevere to the end in faith, hope, and charity, *we beseech you to hear us.*

That you might vouchsafe to hear us, Son of God, *we beseech you to hear us.*

Lamb of God, who take away the sins of the world, *spare us, O Lord.*

Lamb of God, who take away the sins of the world, *graciously hear us, O Lord.*

Lamb of God, who take away the sins of the world, *have mercy on us.*

Versicle: Be glad in the Lord and rejoice, you just.
Response: And glory, all you upright of heart.

Let us pray: We beseech you, O almighty God, through the merits and examples of our most holy Father Saint Benedict, of his disciples Saints Placid and Maur, of his virgin sister Saint Scholastica, and of all the holy monks and nuns who have served you under his standard and guidance, to renew in us your Holy Spirit, that by his inspiration we might strenuously fight against the world, the flesh, and the devil. And since there is no palm of victory without the labor of a contest, grant us patience in adversity, constancy in temptation, and counsel in dangers; give us the purity of chastity, the desire of poverty, the fruit of obedience, and a faithful observance of the regular discipline; that, strengthened by your consolation, we might serve you with united efforts and might so pass through these temporal things as to deserve at length— victoriously crowned and worthy to be associated with the choirs of holy monks—to arrive at our eternal country. Through our Lord Jesus Christ your Son, who lives and reigns with you in the unity of the Holy Spirit, God, world without end. Amen.

BENEDICTINE
PRAYERS

PRAYER TO SAINT BENEDICT TO BRING TO MIND HIS HOLY DEATH

Once, Saint Benedict appeared to Saint Gertrude and instructed her that anyone who would remind him of his glorious death (held erect by his disciples and receiving the Body and Blood of the Lord) would experience his own help at the hour of their death. Benedictines later composed the following prayer to spread devotion to this special help by Benedict.

Antiphon: Benedict, the beloved of the Lord, standing in the oratory, having been fortified with the Body and Blood of the Lord, supporting his failing limbs in the arms of his disciples, with hands upraised to heaven, breathed forth his soul amidst words of prayer, and was seen to ascend to heaven by a way spread with garments and shining with innumerable lamps.

Versicle: You appeared glorious in the sight of the Lord.
Response: Therefore, he clothed you with beauty.

Let us pray: O God, who adorned the precious death of our most holy Father Saint Benedict with so many and so great privileges, grant, we beseech you, that at our departure we may be defended from the snares of the enemy by the blessed presence of him whose memory we celebrate. Through Christ our Lord. Amen.

A FILIAL RECOMMENDATION TO THE MOST BLESSED FATHER SAINT BENEDICT

O most glorious Father Saint Benedict, the governor and leader of those who possess monastic discipline, hope and solace of all who heartily implore your assistance, I humbly recommend myself to your holy protection, that, for the excellence of your merits, you would vouchsafe to defend me from all evils harmful to my soul and that, out of the abundance of your piety, you would obtain for me the gift of compunction and tears, that I may worthily and abundantly bewail my great sinfulness and offenses, with which I have often even in my childhood provoked to anger my loving and gracious Lord Jesus Christ and that I may also worthily praise and reverence you, O most precious olive and fruitful vine in the house of God, most solid vessel adorned with all manner of precious stones, chosen according to God's own heart, most sweet with innumerable gifts of graces, like so many glistening embellished pearls.

You I beseech, you I pray, you with all the affection of my heart, with all the desires of my soul I implore, that you would vouchsafe to be mindful of me, a wretched sinner, with almighty God, that of his infinite goodness he will be pleased to forgive me all my sins, and conserve me in virtues, and that for no cause or necessity whatsoever he will suffer me to depart from him, but that, together with you, O loving Father, he will admit me into the company of his saints and to that blissful vision of himself, where together with you and that glorious army of the religious who have fought under your banner, I may forever enjoy the presence of my God and my Lord Jesus Christ, who with the Father and the Holy Spirit lives and reigns for ever and ever. Amen.

PRAYER ATTRIBUTED
TO SAINT BENEDICT

Faithful and holy Father,
deign to give me
intellect to understand you,
sense to discern you,

a spirit to taste you,
attentiveness to seek you,
wisdom to find you,
a mind to recognize you,
affection to love you,
a heart intent on you,
deeds to exalt you,
ears to hear you,

eyes to see you,
a tongue to proclaim you,
a way of life pleasing to you,
patience to wait for you,
perseverance to look for you,

a perfect end,
your holy presence,
a blessed resurrection,
a heavenly reward,
and eternal life. Amen.

A PRAYER FOR THE INTERCESSION
OF SAINT BENEDICT

Benedict, most illustrious father and guide of monks,
dear to God, inferior in virtue to no saint in all the
world,
you who merited to please Christ according to
your name's foretelling
and established the holy and blessed monastic law:
help me to pursue the remission of my sins.

Righteous shepherd of your holy sheepfold,
rescue me, your ailing sheep, from the jaws of
infernal wolves.
Banish my daily acts of negligence by your holy
prayers.
Turn my soul to love of your precepts and make
my life just.
Direct my acts; purify my thoughts; protect my
body; watch over my soul.

And help me to hold to your precepts daily,
to love you, most righteous father, with all my heart,
despising everything that is opposed to God,
so living in this life that I might escape eternal
punishment
and reach that place where without end you reign
with Christ forever. Amen.

A PENITENTIAL PRAYER
TO SAINT BENEDICT

O holy and most blessed lord and father Benedict,
the Lord has given you to us as our patron, our
shepherd, and our intercessor.

You blessed pauper—gentle, merciful, lover of
peace, filled with every beatitude:
you longed for Christ, and now you live with him
in the fellowship of the blessed apostles Peter, Paul,
and Andrew,
one with the other apostles, martyrs, confessors,
and virgins.

And I—wretched and frail—have sinned in your
courts and in your house with my sinful way of life.

You who are one with the holy apostles, martyrs,
confessors, and virgins,
help me to amend my life and find remission of
sins,
that I might find in turn the Lord's mercy,
leave off my sins, and enter the kingdom of heaven—
lest I perish eternally and proceed to the second death
or the land of oblivion, according to my vices and
sins,

which I—wretched and frail—have done in my
  sinful ways. Amen.

FOR RELATIVES, RULERS, COMMUNITY MEMBERS, FRIENDS, OBLATES, BENEFACTORS, AND ALL WHO ARE CLOSE

PSALM 67

May God have mercy on us, and bless us;
may he cause the light of his countenance to shine
  upon us
and may he have mercy on us.
That we may know your way upon earth,
your salvation in all nations.
Let people confess to you, O God,
let all people give praise to you.
Let the nations be glad and rejoice,
for you judge the people with justice
and direct the nations upon earth.
Let the people, O God, confess to you,
let all the people give praise to you;
the earth has yielded her fruit.
May God, our God, bless us.
May God bless us
and all the ends of the earth fear him.

Glory be to the Father and to the Son and to the
Holy Spirit.

As it was in the beginning, is now, and ever shall
be, world without end. Amen.

Collect

Stretch out your right hand in heavenly aid, O
Lord, to your servants, that they might search
everywhere for you with all their hearts and might
achieve what they worthily pray for. Though Christ
our Lord. Amen.

FOR THE SOULS OF ALL DEPARTED PRELATES, COMMUNITY MEMBERS, RELATIVES, FOUNDERS, BENEFACTORS, OBLATES, OTHER FRIENDS, AND ALL THOSE IN PURGATORY

Psalm 130

Out of the depths I have cried to you, O Lord:

Lord, hear my voice.

Let your ears be attentive to the voice of my
supplication.

If you, O Lord, will mark iniquities,

Lord, who shall stand it?

For with you there is merciful forgiveness,
and by reason of your law I have waited for you, O
Lord.
My soul has relied on his word;
my soul has hoped in the Lord.
From the morning watch even until night,
let Israel hope in the Lord.
Because with the Lord there is mercy,
and with him plentiful redemption.
And he shall redeem Israel from all his iniquities.

Glory be to the Father and to the Son and to the
Holy Spirit.
As it was in the beginning, is now, and ever shall
be, world without end. Amen.

Collect

O God, creator and redeemer of all the faithful,
grant the remission of every sin to the souls of your
servants, that they might obtain that favor which
they ever seek in their holy prayers, you who live
and reign with the Father and the Holy Spirit, God,
for ages unending. Amen.

ACKNOWLEDGMENTS AND PERMISSIONS

Several publishers and others have given me permission and assistance in getting all these prayers together. The Latin text of the three offices from Abbot Ælfwine's prayerbook I translate here appear in the Henry Bradshaw Society volume *Ælfwine's Prayerbook: London, British Library, MS Cotton Titus D.xxvi + xxvii* (London: Henry Bradshaw Society, 1993) by Beate Günzel. Dr. Simon Johnson and Steven Parsons made images of Downside, Abbey Library, MS 26543 available to me for the Commemorations from Winchester's New Minster. The various prayers from Fr. Wendelin Maria Mayer's *St. Benedict's Manual* are reproduced with permission from Verlag Friedrich Pustet. My gratitude goes out to all of you for making these materials available.

My sincerest thanks also go to my best friend and dear wife, Mamie; our three children, Clara, Selevan, and Abram; my brother, Paul; my parents, David and Kim; and all those monastic communities and their oblates who have nurtured my growth in and appreciation of liturgical prayer, especially the Benedictine Sisters of Perpetual Adoration in Clyde, MO; the Camaldolese Benedictines at New Camaldoli Hermitage in Big Sur, CA; the Benedictines at the Monastery of the Ascension in Jerome, ID; the monks at Holy Resurrection Monastery in St. Nazianz, WI; the Benedictines at the Monastero di San Benedetto in Monte in Norcia, Italy; the Benedictines at Stanbrook Abbey in England; and the communities of Kurisumala Ashram and Saccidananda Ashram in southern India. My appreciation also goes to Fr. Cassian Folsom for guidance on finishing this project and for providing a generous foreword. Special thanks for shepherding my Benedictine proclivities go to Sr. Pascaline Coff, Fr. Cyprian Consiglio, and Fr. Hugh Feiss, and to Fr. Bede Griffiths and Dom Henri Le Saux (Swami Abhishiktananda) for most-needed and timely inspiration.

SOURCES

Albers, Bruno. *Consuetudines monasticae.*
    Stuttgart: Roth, 1900–1912.
        A Medieval Little Office of Saint Benedict

Batt, Antonie. *A Poor Man's Mite.* 1639.
        An Early Modern Little Office of Saint
            Benedict
        A Filial Recommendation to the Most
            Blessed Father Saint Benedict

Downside, Abbey Library, MS 26543.
        Commemorations to Be Said after the Divine
            Office

Günzel, Beate. *Ælfwine's Prayerbook.* London:
    Henry Bradshaw Society, 1993.
        The Little Office of the Trinity
        The Little Office of Our Lady
        The Little Office of the Cross
        A Prayer for the Intercession of Saint Benedict
        A Penitential Prayer to Saint Benedict

Mayer, Wendelin Maria. *St. Benedict's Manual.*
    New York: Fr. Pustet, 1891.
        The Little Office of Saint Scholastica
        The Little Office of Saint Gertrude the Great

ABOUT PARACLETE PRESS

WHO WE ARE

As the publishing arm of the Community of Jesus, Paraclete Press presents a full expression of Christian belief and practice—from Catholic to Evangelical, from Protestant to Orthodox, reflecting the ecumenical charism of the Community and its dedication to sacred music, the fine arts, and the written word. We publish books, recordings, sheet music, and video/DVDs that nourish the vibrant life of the church and its people.

WHAT WE ARE DOING

BOOKS | PARACLETE PRESS BOOKS show the richness and depth of what it means to be Christian. While Benedictine spirituality is at the heart of who we are and all that we do, our books reflect the Christian experience across many cultures, time periods, and houses of worship.

We have many series, including *Paraclete Essentials*; *Raven* (fiction); *Iron Pen* (poetry); *Paraclete Giants*; for children and adults, *All God's Creatures*, books about animals and faith; and *San Damiano Books*, focusing on Franciscan spirituality. Others include *Voices from the Monastery* (men and women monastics writing about living a spiritual life today), *Active Prayer*, and new for young readers: *The Pope's Cat*. We also specialize in gift books for children on the occasions of Baptism and First Communion, as well as other important times in a child's life, and books that bring creativity and liveliness to any adult spiritual life.

The MOUNT TABOR BOOKS series focuses on the arts and literature as well as liturgical worship and spirituality; it was created in conjunction with the Mount Tabor Ecumenical Centre for Art and Spirituality in Barga, Italy.

MUSIC | PARACLETE PRESS DISTRIBUTES RECORDINGS of the internationally acclaimed choir *Gloriæ Dei Cantores*, the *Gloriæ Dei Cantores Schola*, and the other instrumental artists of the *Arts Empowering Life Foundation*.

PARACLETE PRESS IS THE EXCLUSIVE NORTH AMERICAN DISTRIBUTOR for the Gregorian chant recordings from St. Peter's Abbey in Solesmes, France. Paraclete also carries all of the Solesmes chant publications for Mass and the Divine Office, as well as their academic research publications.

In addition, PARACLETE PRESS SHEET MUSIC publishes the work of today's finest composers of sacred choral music, annually reviewing over 1,000 works and releasing between 40 and 60 works for both choir and organ.

VIDEO | Our video/DVDs offer spiritual help, healing, and biblical guidance for a broad range of life issues including grief and loss, marriage, forgiveness, facing death, understanding suicide, bullying, addictions, Alzheimer's, and Christian formation.

Learn more about us at our website:
www.paracletepress.com
or phone us toll-free at 1.800.451.5006

SCAN
TO READ
MORE

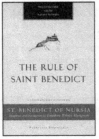